HARRY PICKENS

IN TUNE

LESSONS IN LIFE
FROM A LIFE IN MUSIC

*To Jim, MR. Trumpet,
Keep loving music — and life!
HAPPY BIRTHDAY!
Harry 11.5.2016*

**BUTLER
BOOKS**

This book is dedicated to my grandfather,
HARRY CHARLES CUTHBERT,
whose musical abilities, nobility of character,
and legacy of courage continue to inspire me.
Thank you, Papa.

May these brief essays on music and life
bring you moments of discovery—and may
your life become a living symphony of kindness,
generosity, courage, and compassion.

TALENTS

"Use it or lose it" is Nature's clarion call—
Those gifts and talents left untouched
Might well be none at all.
Through challenge, toil, and steady work—
And practice—day and night,
Untried potentials grow within
And bloom—to bring their light
To all within their radiant grasp.
"What genius!" crowds proclaim!
They have no hint the sacrifice
The discipline, the pains
Those secret hours, the sacred toil
Such efforts we recruit
To bring our seeds of greatness forth
To bear their finest fruit.

—HARRY PICKENS, 1994

Contents

Introduction

THIS BOOK IS FOR MUSIC-MAKERS—ASPIRING, AMATEUR, AND professional—and their teachers, mentors, partners, and friends. It's also for anyone who cares about music and life and wants to nurture the flame of his or her own creative spirit.

In Tune explores eight principles that I believe to be essential for creating a meaningful and fulfilling life—in music and beyond. Each principle is illustrated by a series of short essays. You will find my personal experiences mixed with a few words of wisdom. The principles are:

Purpose: Why getting in touch with your *why* is so important. How discovering my real purpose for making music transformed my life and opened an inner doorway to a realm of boundless creativity, possibility, and joy.

Presence: The underappreciated power of showing up fully—for yourself, for your creative process, for others. Why choosing to fully inhabit the present moment is the first and most fundamental step to becoming a conscious creator of your life experience.

Fundamentals: When in doubt, go back to basics. Don't skip steps. What I learned from Mary Lou Williams, Milt Jackson, and Oscar Peterson about the power of taking one simple step at a time.

Imagination: The master key to, well, everything. How I turned debilitating stage fright into rock-star confidence. How to use your mind to change your brain.

Discipline: There are no shortcuts to putting in the time and doing the work. No grit, no glory. How to outsmart resistance and get stuff done.

Challenge: Failure is your friend. Why learning to constructively deal with failure exponentially increases your capacity for success. The invisible opportunity in every crisis.

Love: In my opinion, love is the ultimate purpose of musical expression. Music as transmission of energy. Becoming an instrument of love.

Teaching: Tributes to inspiring teachers, and a word or two about the teacher's craft.

Each chapter is self-contained, so that you can start anywhere in the book and discover something of value. I didn't write *In Tune* in any particular order, and you don't need to read it from beginning to end. Most chapters started out as Facebook posts; my goal in each was to explore a single topic in a clear, concise, and interesting manner.

I had an insight today as I reviewed the final draft of the manuscript you now hold in your hands (or on your laptop or phone or Kindle). This realization brought a lump to my throat and a tear or two—and revealed to me the deeper reason I wrote *In Tune: Lessons in Life from A Life In Music.*

This is the book I wish I could have read when I was 15, or 18, or 23, or 30.

As a young musician, aspiring to be the best I could become, it would have saved me countless hours in the practice room.

It would have helped me more skillfully navigate the maze of teachers, recordings, mentors, peers, school, gigs, relationships, life.

It would have helped me break free from the prison of my own insecurities and negative thinking.

It would have helped me better see that my unique musical and personal path was not quite like anyone else's, and that the sooner I stopped trying to follow another's path, the sooner I would settle into my own.

It would have helped me begin to trust myself—my inner voice, my heart's wisdom, my deep intuition—more than the well-meaning-but-not-always-relevant advice of others.

It would have helped me see how what I was learning about music also held the keys to my understanding how to create a more harmonious, meaningful, and fulfilling life.

It might have been just the guiding light I needed to keep me from making unwise choices that cost me precious time—time that could never be replaced.

And reading this book might have helped me grasp that music is ultimately not about notes, but about that intangible, ineffable, invisible something that gets transmitted through the notes. I might have discovered sooner that the deeper purpose of music is simply to transmit Love.

Reading this book—especially in high school or college— could have transformed my life. Since I can no longer give these gifts of wisdom to my younger self, I offer them to you.

My deepest desire for you, dear reader, is that something in these pages will touch your heart, stimulate your thinking, inspire you to apply these lessons in your own life, and assist you in fulfilling your own creative potential.

Enjoy.

HARRY PICKENS
August 2016

PART I

In Tune with Purpose

FINDING YOUR WHY

Chapter 1

Look Ma,
No Hands

If you find yourself constantly trying to prove
your worth . . . you have forgotten your value.

—UNKNOWN

I WAS ONLY 22.

Three years after moving to New Jersey to study jazz at Rutgers and get on the inside track in the New York jazz scene, I was rapidly approaching a breaking point.

Although I was making lots of musical progress, excelled in school, and was already getting good gigs with top players—Johnny Griffin, Benny Golson, Art Farmer, and the like—I was absolutely miserable.

It seemed that nothing—musically—would ever be enough.

I never had enough time to practice.

I was never good enough.

I wasn't learning enough tunes.

I didn't know enough patterns, tunes, voicings, and licks.

I was completely stuck in a neurotic and frustrating pattern of self-doubt, self-criticism, and self-sabotage.

Until the dream.

* * *

I have had only three lucid dreams in my life.

You know that kind of dream where everything looks and feels as real as everyday reality?

Some people have lucid dreams practically every night. They have exciting adventures in elaborate, vividly detailed, brightly colored, multisensory alternative universes.

I, on the other hand, rarely remember my dreams, and the ones I do remember tend to be mundane representations of everyday reality, with little color beyond black, white, sepia, or gray.

So you can imagine my shock when I woke up inside a vivid dream that felt as real, if not more real, than my normal waking state. Somehow, I knew I was dreaming in spite of its hyper-reality.

I looked down and was astonished to discover that my hands were gone.

Yes, these were the very same hands that I depended on to play the piano. Cut off at the wrist. I knew there had been no violence involved. No cuts, bruises, or blood anywhere.

Simply an absence of something that had been present before.

I cringed for a moment.

I have no hands. I can't believe this. What happened to my hands? This is weird. I must be dreaming. Am I dreaming? It feels so real.

Then a mysterious calm came over me along with a massive sense of relief.

This was odd. I just discovered I have no hands! I will never be able to play the piano again.

Oh. That's interesting. I just lost the ability to play the piano and I'm not the least bit upset. In fact, all I feel is relief and joy. This is really strange.

Then I got it.

I was relieved that my hands were gone because now I could no longer link my sense of identity and value with how well I played the piano.

In that moment, I realized the source and cause of the neurotic never-enoughness that had been slowly but surely sabotaging my love of music and replacing it with a constant litany of self-criticism, even disdain for my level of ability.

Without hands, I had nothing to prove.

I could relax and enjoy my life. I could finally let go of the obsessive preoccupation with what other people thought of my playing and get on with the business of living.

I could actually enjoy music; even if I could no longer play the piano, I somehow could actually experience and appreciate music more fully—free from the compulsion to compare myself with every Tommy, Dick, and Mulgrew who had ever touched a piano.

I felt a sense of inner peace and tranquility that I had not known for years.

* * *

The dream ended. As I woke up, I immediately looked down at my hands, to make sure they were still there.

Somewhat amazed, I opened and closed my fists, flexed and extended one finger after another, took a good long close look at each hand.

I was so indescribably grateful for these beautiful hands! I felt like Ebenezer Scrooge after his encounter with the three ghosts—strangely liberated, and definitely not the person I was before.

Never again would I invest so much of my sense of value and worth into any external activity.

My value as a human being was not about how well I played—not in the least.

In fact, it was exactly the other way around. I was the one who brought my intrinsic value and worth to the task of making music.

This dream was a gift; the greatest gift I could have ever received at the time.

By "losing" my hands, I found my self.

Chapter 2

Bring on the Funk

Listen to others, but don't lose your own voice.
—ANONYMOUS

YESTERDAY I WAS SPEAKING WITH A FRIEND WHO WAS lamenting the fact that he has not been able to move forward with a recording project for months.

He just turned 50, and has been playing the guitar for decades. Although he doesn't make his living in music (he's a successful entrepreneur), his passion for performance has never waned—until now.

Although he began the project with lots of excitement, it seemed that the more he worked on it, the more he felt drained, tired, frustrated, and embarrassed about not making more progress.

As he continued describing his dilemma, it became clear to me that his relationship to the sheer pleasure of making music had taken a nosedive.

The project he was working on featured jazz and fusion tunes with pretty complex harmonies and intricate rhythms, and it required quite a bit of technical prowess to pull it off.

I asked him, "Is this music fun for you?"

"Fun? Well, not exactly."

"So can you remember a time when you just had an awesome time playing the guitar?"

"Yeah. There was this funk band that I played with for years. I had some of the best times of my life playing that music. You know, '70s grooves like the Ohio Players and Earth Wind and Fire. Oh my gosh, I love that music."

As he kept talking about this music that he loved so much, his speaking became more animated and I could feel the shift in his state of being.

"Tell me more about what you like about this music."

"It just feels so good—and when I had a gig playing with this band back in Toledo, I noticed that we would attract all kinds of people who would come and enjoy the music. They were black and white, young and old, blue-collar and white-collar—the music just really touched them all."

"How long has it been since you played some '70s funk?"

"It's been years."

"So pick up your guitar and play something for me."

He played for a few minutes, an effortless, effervescent joy bubbling up through his hands onto the strings and grooving me right out of my seat!

As the sound faded into silence, he whispered, "Man, that feels good."

"Let's go back to this other music you're working on. Do you even like it?"

"Well, not really. I guess it's what I felt like I should be doing. Kind of like proving to myself that I'm a 'real' musician."

"And neglecting your heart, your soul, and your true musical voice in the process?"

"Maybe."

Our conversation continued.

I told the story of how I was so hooked by the need to please and prove myself to others, that it took me decades to begin to let all of that go and listen to (and honor) my own musical voice.

We talked about the cult of virtuosity, and how many musicians have lost touch with the primal joy of simply sharing music from the heart with others because they are "stuck on show off."

We discussed Herbie Hancock—indisputably one of the finest musicians in the world today—and how he caught hell from critics and many of his colleagues when he recorded *Headhunters* (his first pop-funk album) and branched out into musical genres that could reach the masses.

We explored the elitism so prominent in the jazz and classical worlds, which looks down upon the varieties of "roots" and folk music—from blues to bluegrass to rock to pretty much everything that does not require technical "prowess" and musical "sophistication."

My friend finally realized that the most important thing he could do was to reclaim his core passion for music—by returning to the music he loved—even though it featured no slick chord progressions or intricate technical demands.

He might eventually go back to exploring the other music.

Or he might not.

For now, he is returning to his funk roots with a lighter heart and restored spirit.

Chapter 3

The Wineglass, the Windstorm, and the Will to Thrive

Do everything you can to preserve and protect love so that it endures forever.
—JENNIFER SMITH

I'M HANGING OUT AT RAMSI'S CAFE, MY FAVORITE RESTAURANT in the Highlands neighborhood of Louisville, when I spot her out of the corner of my eye.

She tiptoes ever so slowly across the room.

This obviously inexperienced server with this obviously too full glass of wine is doing everything she can to avoid the spill that is all but inevitable.

Finally, she makes it to the table and carefully places the brimming full glass in front of her guest.

Not a drop is spilled.

Whew.

*   *   *

Three days later, I'm walking down Bardstown Road in Louisville on a balmy Saturday afternoon.

Just as I pass Lilly's restaurant, a sudden wind nearly sweeps me into the wall. Hurricane Ike is on it's way.

By the next morning, Ike's devastating impact is everywhere. Walking in my beloved Cherokee Park, my heart aches as I enter what feels like a war zone, the scattered debris of nature's destructive whim surrounding me.

Mighty maples cracked like toothpicks. Leaves scattered everywhere. An eerie stillness in the air.

*   *   *

It's May of the following year, and I have been invited to provide the commencement address for the University of Louisville School of Music. I'm excited to share a word or two of hard-won wisdom with this next generation of music-makers.

Whenever I have a presentation to make, I ask myself a simple question. What is the single most important, vital, and relevant thing I can share? What one idea will make the greatest possible difference for those I have the privilege to serve?

As I reflect on the glass filled to the brim with wine, and the gale force winds of Ike, I have my answer.

*   *   *

After Dean Doane's introduction, I stride to the podium and turn to address the new graduates.

Those of us who have chosen to build a life in music have one thing in common. We all fell in love. We heard somebody or we saw somebody or we experienced somebody making music, and that was that. It was all over.

We were drawn like bees to honey, like the moth to this flame of beauty and mystery and wonder and all the rest that is the miracle of music.

In this first magical moment, we begin to fill the glass of our heart with a most intoxicating wine. This is the wine of our pure and unabashed love of music. It is a wine of innocent delight, of unrefined passion, of naive but total surrender.

Our glass is soon filled to the brim. And now we can begin to generously share this delicious refreshment with others. They, too, can drink of our joy.

As we begin the long and arduous journey towards mastery, however, we begin to encounter powerful winds.

"No, you can't play those songs you like—not until you learn this way."

"The recital is coming up. Are you practicing?"

"You need to put in the work every day. That's what it means to be a real musician."

Then more winds begin to blow as we meet the inevitable challenges we are bound to face as we move forward.

The disciplinarian teachers who insist that we follow their paths and focus only on their preferred genre of music, and who compare us to their other students, and who look for us to gratify their egos.

The never-ending pressures of lessons and practice and recitals.

The daily discipline, dedication, determination it takes to keep going whether you feel like it or not. The constant drive to improve, to excel, to succeed.

Then, should you choose a music major in college, storm winds begin to blow.

"You're obviously a talented student, but you're in college now, and it's going to be very different from high school. You are no longer a big fish in a little pond. Everyone is at least as talented as you are. Get used to it.

You can't just focus on your performance skills. There's music theory, and music history, and ensembles, and sight-singing, and ear training.

And don't forget—you've got general education requirements to fulfill—English composition, biology, geography, history, and more.

Plus you'll have to prepare for your juries. Let's get to work."

The required non-music classes that we have no interest in. The theory and history and ear training and literature and extra rehearsals and uninspired professors and competitive, jealous peers, and financial aid and course registration nightmares, and on and on and on.

The music school hurricane.

And suppose we make it through music school with our wineglass still full, our love and passion fully intact.

More winds.

"I've got my degree, so how do I find a job?"

"How am I going to earn a living?"

"Can I stay in music and survive?"

"I'm getting a lot of pressure to do something else. Maybe a life in music really isn't for me. What are my options? Starbucks?"

Ouch.

We next encounter the never-ending winds of uncertainty, of financial insecurity, of tough career choices, of a society that rarely embraces artists and creators with open arms.

All along, we do our best to keep the wine in the glass, but inevitably, some begins to spill.

Our passion for the sheer delight of music making begins to wane.

Music begins to feel like more job than joy.

We begin to question ourselves, our abilities, our love for music in the first place.

My fellow musicians, I believe your most important task now, like that of the server at Ramsi's Café, is to keep your wineglass full.

Even in the face of the winds that will threaten to destroy it, your first objective must be to present and preserve your essential, foundational, fundamental love and passion for music.

Only then will you be able to fully and freely share the miracle of music with others.

Only then will you be able to pass on the indescribable fulfillment that is the musicians' birthright.

Only then will you feel the deep delight and boundless joy of a life in music.

The winds will continue.

Keep your wineglass full.

Chapter 4

The Cure for Stage Fright

Give what you have. To someone,
it may be better than you dare to think.
—HENRY WADSWORTH LONGFELLOW

VINCENT VAN GOGH WAS HANGING OUT IN HIS APARTMENT, writing a letter to his brother, Theo Gogh (a.k.a. Bro Gogh). He paused for a sec, looked up and out the window, and noticed a huge full moon that knocked his socks off. (Of course, Vincent van G. probably wasn't wearing socks, but you never know.)

He thought to himself—*Self, this is some awesome sky tonight. And the way the moonlight illuminates that streetlamp! Where's my camera phone? Oops, smartphones haven't been invented yet. Hmm. I guess I'll have to—draw it! Yep. I'll draw this thing.*

So he turns the letter over on the backside and draws a classic van Gogh-ish sketch of the full moon, the stars, the streetlamp. At the bottom of the sketch, he writes: "Yo, Theo, dude—I just had to share this with you because it is so beautiful."

Then he flips the page back over and finishes the letter. Presses send (oops, sorry, email wasn't invented then, either); snail mails it to Bro. T.

And herewith thou shalt discover the *ultimate cure* for performance jitters. You know, those oh-too-familiar thoughts that tie you up in nervous knots when it's your turn to make music in front of others.

"I had to share this with you because it is so beautiful."

Van Gogh drew the picture because he was struck by the incredible beauty of that moonlit night and wanted to share it with someone he loved.

His motivation was not to draw a sketch that would put dollars in his pocket. He wasn't concerned about his brother evaluating his sketch for perfection of form or perspective or accuracy. (Although brother Theo did happen to be an art dealer and undoubtedly understood those things, including how to make a shekel or two.)

Nope. Vincent just wanted to share something beautiful with someone he cared about.

Why can't our experience of making music be the same? What would happen if, every time we were to play or sing, we were just sharing something beautiful with people we care about?

It's like Gramma's apple cobbler. (Stay with me here—this is all coming back to music in a minute. I'm not desserting you . . . well, maybe I am. Yum.)

She spends the whole day going to the store, cutting up the apples, mixing the crust, and baking the cobbler. When you go over to her house for dinner, and its dessert time, what does she say?

"Here, honey, have some cobbler!" And you munch out. When that cobbler hits your mouth, Gramma is not on your mind. I mean, it's nice that she cared about you enough to make it, but your mind is on the yum-yum. Then you take another piece. And another. And you stagger home on a sugar high.

Although you thank Gramma for cooking it (I hope you thanked her—where *are* your manners?), while you are eating the cobbler, Gramma's not on your mind.

Nope. It's all about the apples, the cinnamon, the crunchy melt-in-your-mouth crust, the sheer deliciousness of it all.

Also, *you* are not on your mind. Neither are you thinking about anyone else who is gathered around that table. (I know, nobody gathers around tables to eat anymore. They sit staring at their phones while munching on fast food GMO pseudo-meals. But humor me, okay?)

In that moment, you couldn't care less what others are thinking. Do they like your haircut? Do they approve of your appetite? Do they care about the food dripping down your neck? (Well, maybe they do care about that. Whatever.)

Nope. You're not looking for approval. Not in this moment.

All of your attention is focused on the cobbler.

*　*　*

When you were a little kid, you probably at some point in your life found something outside that you thought was really cool—a flower, a frog, a rock, a worm.

You got excited about this thing, ran inside, and showed it to your mom, dad, big brother, or sis.

You said—look at this thing? Ain't it cool?

And they said *wow*, or they screamed *"Where did you get that? Give that to me and go wash your hands right now!"*

Or they said, "Oh yeah. That's a cool whatchamagig. Now go back outside and play."

In that instant, your attention was not on yourself or on them. Your attention was focused on this thing of beauty (or at least of interest) that you found and wanted to share because it was cool.

What if your experience of sharing music was the same way?

What if you approached performance not as an egocentric display or a form of medieval torture where everyone in the audience was there to think badly of you?

What if it wasn't about you at all?

What if it was simply an opportunity to say to someone—hey, check out this Beethoven dude. Amazing stuff!

Can you believe this Monk? This is awesome! Check out this Chopin. Can you believe how beautiful this is?

Here. Have some cobbler. Yeah. It's really good. Yum. I knew you'd like it.

What if the very act of sharing music was simply that—sharing something cool and beautiful and interesting and awesome with someone you care about?

"I just had to share this with you because it is so beautiful."

Just like van Gogh.

Just like Gramma's cobbler.

Just like the frog, or the rock, or the flower.

Chapter 5

Life, Death, and the Meaning of Music

You matter because you are you,
and you matter to the end of your life.
—DAME CICELY SAUNDERS, FOUNDER
OF THE HOSPICE MOVEMENT

"WHAT WOULD YOU LIKE TO HEAR?"

"I don't know. I like hymns. How about 'Amazing Grace'?"

"What can I play for you?"

"Well, I really love Gershwin."

"What's your favorite?"

"Chopin."

"Would you play 'You Are My Sunshine'? Daddy used to sing it to me when I was little."

Over the past several years, I have had the privilege of being with a number of people who were facing their final days of life.

Beyond the sorrow, the grief, the heartache, I discovered a place of consolation, comfort, even joy.

That place was not accessed through the mind or through conversation, or even through prayer (although perhaps this entire chapter is really about a certain kind of prayer).

I didn't plan to arrive at this place of inner serenity and profound gratitude, but nonetheless found myself there.

The means of this experience of grace? Music.

In each case, I simply sat in the presence of these beloved friends and played the piano.

* * *

Roger used to come to my concerts at the University of Louisville. He often sat in the front row with his kids. I hadn't seen him for several years when his daughter, now grown, sent me an email.

"Dad's in the last stages of liver cancer. He doesn't have very long. Would you be willing to come over to the house and play for him for a little while? Dad always loved your concerts."

I drove over to Roger's suburban home a few days later. He was emaciated and quite weak, but his smile lit up the room when our eyes met.

I walked over and sat down at the piano, beginning to thumb through the stack of music books on the piano bench beside me.

"So Roger, I know you like jazz, but do you have any requests? I see lots of classical and show tunes in this stack. I'll play anything you want—if I know it."

"I really love Gershwin."

"Well, Gershwin it is."

For nearly an hour, I played tune after tune scribed by George and Ira.

"Somebody Loves Me."

"I've Got Rhythm."

"'S Wonderful."

"How Long Has This Been Going On?"

"Love Walked In."

"Embraceable You."

"Prelude #2 in C# Minor."

"Nice Work If You Can Get It."

"Someone to Watch Over Me."

And finally—"Our Love Is Here To Stay."

Roger sat back and closed his eyes for most of this informal private concert.

When I finished, his eyes glistening with tears, he simply whispered, "Thank you so much."

"You're so welcome, Roger. I love you."

A hug for everyone (his wife and daughter were there, too) and I was on my way.

I got to the car and couldn't drive away. I had to just sit, eyes closed, for a moment of reflection and gratitude.

Wow. That was the last time I will see Roger. I am so grateful that she asked me to play for him. What a blessing to share music in this way.

Thank you, Creator.

* * *

Carol had been in a coma at home for weeks. A mutual friend, who used to bring her to many of my house concerts, told me that one of her last wishes, before she lost consciousness, was for me to play for her. Unfortunately, when I found out about Carol's condition, I was out of town and wouldn't be back in Louisville for a week.

When I returned home, I got in touch with Carol's son, who told me she was still alive, but quickly fading. I went over to her apartment that very afternoon, keyboard in tow.

Carol was lying on the bed, her breath labored, eyes closed, seemingly unresponsive.

But I went up to her anyway.

I touched her gently on the shoulder.

"Carol, it's Harry. Thanks for waiting for me to get back home. I love you and have something for you—some music to help you on your journey."

I played for about an hour—mostly improvising, a few quieter standards and hymns that I knew she liked. Then, after about 30 minutes, I felt a tangible shift in the room. The music that flowed through me became quite sparse and slowed down—almost to stillness. By the time I finished, I felt a strange and sacred silence filling the room. I just sat there quietly for a moment.

Then I picked up my keyboard, nodded wordlessly to her son as I walked out the door, and returned home.

Three hours later, I received a phone call. "Harry, Carol passed about an hour after you left. It's like she was waiting for you before she could say goodbye."

I believe the music actually did help her finally say goodbye to this life and hello to the mystery that follows.

What a privilege to have the opportunity to share music in such a raw, vulnerable, and simple form.

* * *

I've done this perhaps a dozen times now. I never play anything too fancy, virtuosic, or profound. Folk songs. Hymns. Standards sometimes. Often I just create simple improvisations that come from a heart humbled by the opportunity to serve.

In every case, I left the person's bedside with my heart

strangely warmed. Filled with a deep knowing that, in those moments, I did exactly what I was put on this planet to do.

Surprisingly, I noticed that these simple acts of musical service meant more to me—felt somehow more fulfilling—than performing on some of the largest and most prestigious stages on earth.

If you are a musician (pro or amateur), I invite you to explore this simple act of service. (Of course, my friends in music therapy do this for a living—they 'get' the transcendent power of music as an agency of healing love perhaps more than the rest of us.)

Play or sing for one person.

Just one.

And it doesn't even have to be someone who's dying.

That may be the case, or if that's too intense for you for now, simply play or sing for an older person—maybe your grandparent or aunt or uncle or neighbor.

Or play or sing a love song to your sweetheart.

Or play or sing for a friend who's having a rough time.

Sharing music one on one is, for me, one of the most powerful, profound, and life-transforming ways to truly 'get' what a miracle music can be.

And when you start to feel that *you* are the instrument—an instrument of love, beauty, healing—you have finally begun to glimpse music's true power.

Chapter 6

Music as a Force for Good

You may say I'm a dreamer, but I'm not the only one.
—JOHN LENNON

I WROTE THIS LETTER A FEW YEARS AGO TO A PROFOUNDLY gifted young musician about the astonishing opportunity we each have to be a force for good in the world. I am honoring through this publication a request to share it more widely.

My dear reader, please imagine this letter is addressed to you.

Dear Friend,

I have been thinking of you and thinking about your musical future and destiny and felt a strong desire to share a few thoughts with you . . .

Please read this letter slowly, pondering each idea. I am happy to discuss these in depth with you whenever you are ready.

I offer this to you as your friend, mentor, guide, in service to you becoming the very best you that you can and helping to change this world for the better.

You are a leader. A leader is simply someone who cares about people and the planet and is willing to step up, take a stand, and inspire people to take action in service of a better community, nation, and planet.

Your gift of music is one of the greatest tools in existence for leading people into a new way of seeing, thinking, being, acting in the world.

You yield tremendous influence over others—whether you realize it or not—and this brings tremendous responsibility.

You can lead people through your music into new possibilities, opening their hearts and minds to feel things and see things they never realized were possible before.

Music is an amplifier of your state of consciousness and awareness; therefore, the more fully and completely you develop as a human being, the more powerful and transformational your music will become for those who experience it.

The gift of music is a sacred trust. Your ability to touch people's hearts is a holy gift. Regardless of your spiritual beliefs, you engage in a spiritual endeavor every time you play and sing. Always remember that music is sacred, whether it's heard in a bar, a classroom, or a cathedral.

You have just barely begun to realize the full extent of your talents and gifts. You are just beginning a journey that could bring you not only external success, but most importantly, a degree of inner fulfillment and an opportunity to make a real and positive impact in the world.

Devote yourself fully and with your whole soul to becoming the very best musician, vocalist, and songwriter you can become.

Study both the art and craft of music making.

Expose yourself to the very best teachers, role models, and examples of excellence you can find.

Dedicate yourself to the highest degree of excellence that you can conceive.

Music is perhaps one of the most powerful tools for catalyzing social change. Both the South African liberation movement and the American Civil Rights movement were powered through song.

Musicians and artists have traditionally been on the front lines for social justice, from Woody Guthrie and Joan Baez to John Coltrane and Charles Mingus, from Pete Seeger, Odetta, and Sweet Honey in the Rock to the millions of anonymous slaves singing coded spirituals that led the way towards freedom, and many countless others in practically every nation on earth. Every significant social movement in human history has gained momentum and strength through the power of tone, sound, rhythm, and music.

As a musician and performer, you have the ears and hearts of people who otherwise would not listen to what you have to say. You will have in your audience rich and poor; black, white, and brown; educated and illiterate; accountants and artists; entrepreneurs and day laborers—every color, culture, class, and creed—the full spectrum of the human family.

You alone—more than the politicians, the business people, the academics—have the power to bring these wildly divergent folks together in a spirit of unity, of harmony, of compassion, and belief in a better future. Use this power!

Talk to your audiences—during shows, through email, social media, in your albums—about your highest vision for humanity, about the power of love, and about how we can build a fabulous, sustainable, just, peaceful world for everyone if we will all come together.

Your songs could become many people's soundtrack for their lives.

What ideas can you share that will turn their minds and hearts towards the good? What songs will you write and perform that will uplift, inspire, empower, and mobilize them, enrich their lives, and feed their hope? What is the single most important idea that you would hope people will think about and act upon after they hear you perform?

My dear, beloved friend, you wield such power with your voice and your guitar. Always remember: it is the artist who holds the future of the people in his or her hands.

It is the artist whose sensitivity to both the deep suffering and profound joy of existence compels them to create works that will open hearts and eyes and minds.

It is the artist whose vision of a better, truer existence penetrates every barrier of belief, doubt, and defensiveness, to directly enter the very heart of humanity and call forth a better world.

Never forget how important a role you can play in the transformation of this planet.

Begin thinking now about who you want to reach, about the message you choose to share, about the influence you want to have.

Bring together great, honest, humble, devoted, smart people to help you manifest your vision.

Learn everything you can about the creative process, about awakening your spiritual capacities, about becoming the most fabulous version of yourself you can imagine.

And give yourself fully to Life itself. Live, love, laugh, be luminous with joy, and leave a legacy of hope for all who follow you.

My dear, dear beloved (and new—but so, so old) friend, you have a rainbow of treasures within. Now is the time for you to release them to a ready and hungry world.

With deep and enduring love,

Harry

PART II

In Tune with Presence

SHOWING UP FULLY

Chapter 7

Twenty-Four Hours to Live

Look to this day, for it is Life
The very Life of Life.

—SALUTATION TO THE DAWN

EIGHT FORTY-FIVE TUESDAY MORNING. THE PHONE RINGS.

"Hello?"

"Harry, this is Donna. Did you hear about Bob?"

My heart sank. Bob had been dealing with loads of health problems, most recently with his heart, and just the past Sunday, he mentioned that he wasn't doing so well. A new medication was making him drowsy and he was feeling out of sorts.

"He had a heart attack last night—he's gone."

Bob and I had only known each other for a few months, but we had become fast friends. In fact, in our last telephone conversation just a few days before, he had been describing how his spiritual life was blossoming. "I am feeling so much love. I wonder why it took me 60 years to realize how much love is really available. My heart is just full of gratitude."

A few months after Bob's passing, I was preparing to head to Idyllwild, California, to perform at the Jazz in the Pines music festival, a two-day musical fest held every August in this idyllic mountain town just a few miles east of Los Angeles. Idyllwild has to be one of the most beautiful places on earth, nearly six thousand feet above sea level, and home to many outstanding artists, musicians, writers, actors, and other creative exemplars.

The Friday night before my performance, I was staying in Hemet, a desert town just 20 miles away. I was awakened before dawn by a particularly vivid dream.

In my dream, Bob appeared. I am shopping in Kroger's supermarket, pushing a cart full of groceries down the aisle, and Bob comes around the corner walking towards me. I'm thrilled, because I never had the opportunity to say goodbye. "Hey, Bob! How are you doing, my friend?" I move forward to embrace him.

Bob stops in his tracks, looks me straight in the eyes, and says, "You're next. You have 24 hours."

I snapped awake, stunned, shocked, startled.

Oh my God.

Bob just told me I'm going to die.

This is my last day on earth. The dream—and the message—were so vivid, so clear.

I have not seen or thought of Bob in months, and there he is, showing up just to deliver this message.

What should I do? I'm not ready to die. I'm only 37 years old. I have so much of life ahead. This isn't fair. Maybe it's not true. But maybe it is. Should I even get out of bed? Well, I have to. I have to play this afternoon at the festival. Maybe I should call them and say something happened and I have to cancel. That would be crazy. Maybe I'm going to die in a car crash.

Twenty-four hours?

That means today is my last day on earth.

Wow.

Bob, why did you wait until now to tell me?

* * *

I didn't know what to do. It was just a silly dream. It was not real.

But it felt real.

I rarely remember my dreams, so when I do, it means one of two things: Either I ate onion rings the night before (onion rings always give me vivid nightmares), or the dream is happening for a reason and must have a message.

Okay, did I have onion rings last night? No.

Okay. Obviously, this was a prophetic dream and I am going to die—maybe today. Or sometime tomorrow. Wow.

I stumbled out of bed, took a shower, and steeled myself for the inevitable. This was my last 24 hours on earth.

Then something really weird happened.

My brain shut off. My mind went quiet.

I started noticing things—the floral pattern of the carpet in the Best Western hotel room; the billowy clouds set against the bright blue Southern California desert sky; the tart taste of the oatmeal I usually gulped down too fast to notice.

I went to Rite-Aid to buy a tube of toothpaste. There was an older lady in the line in front of me and when she got to the counter, she needed to dig deep into her cavernous purse for change. In the past, I would have been inwardly fuming with impatience, judging and convicting this stranger on 10 counts of age-related slowness in the court of my mind.

Not today. I felt only love and compassion for this unique, beautiful human being in front of me, knowing that the one thing we certainly had in common was that our lives would end one day.

The rest of the morning, this state of expanded and expansive present-moment awareness continued. I was a bit anxious driving up Highway 74 to Idyllwild, wondering if a fatal accident would lead to my final exit. At the same time, the pine-tree-lined road up the mountain never looked so stunningly beautiful.

* * *

I arrived safely in Idyllwild and drove straight to the performance venue. Last performance ever. I might as well give it my best.

I noticed that I was connecting with people as though this really was the last time I would ever see them. Looking directly in their eyes. Being fully present instead of half-attending to them while my mind wandered on to the next thing. Noticing, caring, really listening to what was going on for them.

I kept the dream secret, because I didn't want to upset anyone. And yet, all day that Saturday, I walked in absolute certainty that it was my last day on earth.

The performance was transcendent. Marshall Hawkins, the living legend bassist in my trio, broke down in tears at the end of our hour-long set. The standing-room-only audience leapt to their feet. And as I took a bow, the sense that this was really the last time flooded through my awareness.

The rest of the day and evening, I did my best to savor each moment and enjoy just being with my friends and fans, my heart breaking with this news that I could not and would not share.

That night, my head hit the pillow. I surrendered. I was

relieved to have made it through the day and did not expect to wake on Sunday morning.

* * *

I have never felt quite as relieved and thankful as I did that next morning. It took a few days for the realization to truly settle in that perhaps my death was not as imminent as I supposed.

Over time, I became aware that I had been given a truly priceless gift.

Bob's message—"You're next. You have 24 hours"—I now see not so much as a dire warning but as a loving reminder.

"You're next."

In our final conversation, which took place just days before Bob's sudden death, he spoke with wonder about a spiritual awakening he was experiencing, an expansive sense of gratitude for the unrepeatable miracle of life.

I was given a glimpse of this gratitude in my 24-hour journey.

Now, nearly two decades later, I finally understand Bob's message. I was next, just as he told me. I did get a tiny glimpse of what Bob was describing in his last days on earth.

And I do have only 24 hours at a time. I have only this day to live. To appreciate. To savor. To give thanks. To love. To be.

This day, this moment—this is all any of us ever really have.

The next moment, the next heartbeat, the next breath is never guaranteed.

For 24 golden hours, I had the opportunity to live this grace and gratitude as my embodied, experiential reality.

I have never been the same.

Thank you, Bob.

Chapter 8

Speaking in Notes

The purpose of jazz is joy.
—HARRY "SWEETS" EDISON

WALTER BEGAN BY PLAYING THE OPENING THEME OF BUD Powell's tune "Oblivion," continuing with a note-for-note-perfect replication of Bud's solo. His raspy voice sang in impeccable synchrony with his right hand as it danced along the keys with delightful abandon.

"Then, on 'Dance of the Infidels,' Bud said . . ."

Walter's demonstration continued, the living spirit of Bud Powell pouring itself through his hands with an effervescent intensity that nearly took my breath away.

This musical ritual continued for the next two hours—"Glass Enclosure," "Hallucinations," "Un Poco Loco," "The Fruit," "Parisian Thoroughfare"—all for an audience of one, a 23-year-old, tall, lanky Georgia pianist brand new to the New York scene. I was hungry to absorb every word, note, and idea uttered by this living legend sitting at this slightly out-of-tune spinet piano.

What I noticed the most—besides the astonishing

musicianship on display—was how Walter talked about Bud's playing. He never said Bud played this note, this phrase, this chord, this progression.

It was always, "Bud said this" and "Bud said that."

Speaking his truth. Telling his story. Music as language.

Pure, undiluted self-expression.

I never had seen so clearly the absolute and direct and unbroken connection between heart, head, and hands. The music was clearly bubbling up from a place inside Walter that was deeper than any ocean I had ever imagined.

He simply became the music in every cell of his body.

He was the music. There was no separation between his essence and the music pouring forth from within.

He embodied the sound, the phrasing, the joy, the swing, the machine-gun-like propulsive intensity that was Bud Powell.

It was all there, in this tiny studio on the Lower West Side where this master of all things bebop, Mr. Walter Davis Jr., had agreed to meet me for a two-hour piano lesson.

For most of these two hours (which seemed to last both for an eternity and for a nanosecond), I simply sat and watched as Walter played tune after tune, impeccably demonstrating Bud's voicings, phrasing, and articulation.

The reason I approached him in the first place?

I knew that he had known Bud personally. As a teenager, he had also had the remarkable opportunity to play with saxophonist Charlie Parker. Since I was at the time utterly obsessed with learning everything I possibly could about this jazz piano icon, I was hanging around everyone and anyone who had touched the hem of Bud's bop garment.

And of all the pianists living at that time, Walter was the

one, for my ears, who most powerfully captured the essence and spirit of Bud Powell's particular brand of bebop.

I remember a solo piano concert at Douglass Chapel on the Rutgers University campus in New Brunswick. Walter's set of jazz standards and Powell originals forever transformed my idea of solo jazz piano. It wasn't just the effortless virtuosity and relentless swing; it was the spiritual light, the youthful spontaneity, and the vibrant effervescence that emanated from this man's soul.

Head held back, his face glowing with delight and surprise as the music took its own twists and turns, his lips constantly moving as he hummed along, Walter Davis was a man whose body, mind, and heart simply dissolved into pure music before my eyes.

One night in the early 1980s, I went up to the loft that housed the Jazz Forum in New York City to bear witness to what was the ultimate bebop piano collaboration at the time: Barry Harris and Walter Davis.

Now, Barry Harris is a master by anyone's assessment. I always have and always will admire and respect Barry's lyrical touch, musical impeccability, lift-you-out-of-your-seat swing, and absolute, total commitment to being a keeper of the bebop flame. This man is a monster musician by any standard. Hearing these two master pianists face off took me right to musical heaven.

From the first note of the first tune, Charlie Parker's "Ornithology," Walter and Barry tossed idea after idea back and forth with childlike glee.

As amazing as Barry's playing was, it was Walter's shimmering swing that touched me the most. He combined an authoritative mastery of the bop language with an intensity, joy, and pure presence that I will never forget.

I learned more about the essence of music in those priceless two hours with this man who was a pure embodiment of the spirit of jazz than I did in all the times I spent studying music in the classroom combined.

Thank you, Walter.

Chapter 9

Goode Healing

Music is a therapy. It is a communication far more powerful than words, far more immediate, far more efficient.
—YEHUDI MENUHIN

I WAS FEELING AWFUL THAT DAY.

I had been ill for more than a year with the aftereffects of toxic mold poisoning.

For me, at the time, a good day meant I had at best a couple hours of almost normal energy; on a bad day, I could barely get out of the bed. I was emaciated, weak, tired, and depressed most of the time.

This Sunday afternoon was no exception. But I wanted to hear him play.

Richard Goode was a pianistic legend, particularly for his powerful interpretations of Beethoven. Since I knew his appearance in Louisville would likely be a once-in-a-lifetime occurrence, I dragged myself to Comstock Concert Hall that Sunday afternoon.

It was one of the best decisions I would ever make.

As expected, Mr. Goode's playing was impeccable, sensitive, imbued with delicate yet fierce beauty. His interpretations of Schubert and Bach were outstanding.

But it was his Beethoven that stunned me.

(It also opened a portal to the healing I so desperately needed—but never would have expected to experience at a piano recital. More on that later.)

* * *

They gasped in astonishment.

Never before had the world known such a passionate and unpredictable, yet brilliant improviser.

There was no distance, no gap between inspiration and execution in his mind or his fingers. The instant he felt an impulse, it was translated into sound.

And each of his timeless compositions was born from this unique musical mind that perfectly integrated the immediacy of the improviser with the architectural mastery of the skilled craftsman.

The depth and beauty of Beethoven's spontaneous musical expressions are lost to history now. Yet, we still can experience the thrill of bearing witness to this process of instantaneous musical invention.

As an improvising pianist, I have some insight into how a person can create quality music on the fly. Massive preparation has to occur. Countless hours of practice and deep familiarity with the elements of composition are necessary.

And the payoff for all that hard work? The feeling is unequalled.

In the best moments, it is as though one becomes a living, breathing instrument of music itself, a hollow reed through which the Creative Intelligence animating all life may speak, sing, and sound.

* * *

I don't recall which sonata he played, but it really doesn't matter.

What astonished me was that it seemed that he was channeling the living spirit of Beethoven.

It's hard to describe exactly what occurred as I watched and listened to this man play the piano. It felt like he was improvising, as though this centuries' old masterpiece was literally being created in this moment, right there, on the stage, in front of me and the others present.

A time warp occurred. Beethoven was no longer a composer who was born in 1770 and died in 1827. No. He was alive now. Fully present and resonant in this moment.

At some point, as I more deeply surrendered to the over-whelming intensity of this tonal transmission, Goode was gone.

He had become utterly transparent to the sounds that thundered through him.

In fact, there was no more piano, no more concert hall, no more audience, no me.

There was only music, perpetually and spontaneously giving birth to more and more of itself in each and every unrepeatable moment.

And then it happened.

I felt an odd yet familiar sensation all through my body as I melted into music.

It was uncanny.

I had experienced hands-on healing, qi gong, Reiki, and other modalities wherein an invisible power—energy, prana, qi—is evoked and activated for the purposes of physical, emotional, or spiritual healing.

Now I was feeling the exact same surge of energy moving

through my cells as I bore witness to Beethoven's resurrection through the instrumentality of Richard Goode.

I would never forget this concert. And I would never forget the way my physical body felt after experiencing nearly two hours of this remarkable sonic infusion.

I felt better than I had for months.

Clear, present, energized, no sense of weakness or exhaustion.

This radiant state of being sustained itself for several days.

I had experienced firsthand the healing power of music, thanks to Mr. Beethoven and Mr. Goode.

What a miracle.

Perhaps Beethoven understood this possibility.

He once wrote, "Music is the mediator between the spiritual and the sensual life."

And it did seem as though the pure energy of inspiration that moved through Beethoven as he created this sonata somehow transmitted itself through the living human antenna that was Richard Goode, then traveled through the air and into my body to restore me to greater harmony and wholeness.

Thank you, Mr. Beethoven.

Thank you, Mr. Goode.

What startling power music wields in the hands of its humble and devoted servants.

Chapter 10

Bill Evans at the Vanguard

Music is a holy place, a cathedral so majestic that we can sense the magnificence of the universe, and also a hovel so simple and private that none of us can plumb its deepest secrets.

—DON CAMPBELL

I HAD NEVER BEFORE EXPERIENCED A CONCERT VENUE transform into a cathedral. Even when I attended symphony concerts in great concert halls. Even when I heard chamber music performed by some of the greatest musicians alive. Even when I sat in the auditorium at Brevard Music Center bearing witness to the musical miracles that were André Watts, Leonard Pennario, and Andre-Michel Schub.

Nothing I heard previously, either live or recorded, prepared me for the simple yet profound spiritual presence I felt that Sunday afternoon in 1980 at the Village Vanguard in the presence of the Bill Evans Trio.

I was sitting fewer than five feet away from the piano, ready to make my single glass of orange juice last for the entire set.

And there they were.

Bill Evans, Joe LaBarbera, and Marc Johnson.

From the moment they came on stage, they cast a spell.

Not one word was spoken by any member of the trio during the entire set. In fact, after the opening announcement and welcome, not one word was spoken by anyone in the room during the entire set.

The silence beneath the sound reflected an intensity of listening, of presence, of attention, of awareness that I had rarely experienced in a public place. I had often entered into this kind of contemplative reverie on my own, but only when listening to music by myself or with a select group of friends.

The world's great mystical literature often refers to the ultimate spiritual goal of entering fully into the present moment, experiencing the eternal now, describing how the mind's chatter can go so silent that only pure consciousness remains.

I don't know if this is what I was glimpsing as I sat in the Vanguard that afternoon, but whatever my soul was tasting was utterly new and delightful to me. No thought or mental commentary could possibly survive the wave after wave of sonic light that began to wash over me.

For one holy hour, the Vanguard became a sacred space, a place where the music of Bill Evans invited and evoked an energy of transcendence that I must refer to as divine.

Evans, Johnson, and LaBarbera no longer appeared to be three separate musicians. They were playing as one, each now an instrument expressing the singular will of a loving, gentle, yet powerful muse.

All were caught up in Evans's reverie. There was an intensity and purity to his concentration that I had not experienced in a jazz performance before. No separation whatsoever between man, heart, hands, music. Only a single seamless unity of mind, body, spirit, soul, and sound.

I hung on to every note, every phrase, every chord, every moment of this spontaneous musical miracle unfolding before my eyes and ears. I didn't know many of the tunes, and this lack of familiarity prompted me to listen even more deeply. Every moment brought new surprises, new discoveries, unexpected twists and turns in this sonic journey without a destination.

When the set was over, my mind was empty, my heart full, my spirit aloft.

For the first time, I experienced jazz as sacred art, and understood that this form of spontaneous music making could express the widest range of human sentiment as well as human aspiration.

I knew now that it was possible to create a shared sacred space through only music—no words, no ritual, no dogma, no ideology necessary.

The music was enough.

Less than one year later, Evans was dead. This was to be his last performance at the Vanguard.

Thank you, Bill Evans, for this glimpse of eternity.

PART III

In Tune with Fundamentals

HANDLING THE BASICS

Chapter 11

Mary Lou Williams Set Me Straight

*The vision must be followed by the venture. It is not enough
to stare up the steps—we must step up the stairs.*

—VANCE HAVNER

AFTER NO MORE THAN 30 SECONDS, SHE STOPPED ME.

"That's nice. You can blow. But you need to go back to the roots. Do you know about Fats Waller?"

That day, Mary Lou Williams taught me a great lesson.

One that applies to much more than music.

She taught me not to skip steps.

*   *   *

I met her only one time.

It was the summer of 1980. I was visiting Duke University as a National Endowment for the Arts artist-in-residence. Since Ms. Williams lived in Durham, I couldn't pass up the opportunity to be in her presence and learn from this musical icon.

Honestly, I was disappointed.

Not in her or in her teaching abilities.

Not in the least.

I was disappointed because I only got to play the piano for maybe three minutes that afternoon.

I was a cocky 20-year-old kid who wanted to show off my chops.

And I had been obsessively studying the bebop language, particularly the music of Bud Powell, for the previous year or so.

"So play me some blues, young man."

I lit into a version of "Dance of the Infidels" that was about twice the recorded tempo.

I played so fast partially because I was scared to death. Plus, I wanted to show off.

Alas, my 20-year-old ego was soon dealt a crushing blow.

Ms. Williams stopped me in the middle of my second chorus.

"Okay. That's fine. You can blow. You like Bud, don't you?"

"Yes, ma'am."

"I taught Bud Powell—and Monk, too."

"Now show me what you can do with your left hand. Do you know Teddy Wilson? Nat Cole? Fats Waller? Art Tatum?"

I responded weakly, "I have listened to them, but not very much."

The matronly Ms. Williams looked at me with great kindness. Then she laid it out.

"You need to go back to Fats Waller."

Fats Waller? I thought. "Ain't Misbehavin'" Fats Waller? You mean that hokey, corny stride stuff? Come on, aren't you impressed with my bebop? I can play even faster. Are you seriously telling me to study Fats Waller?

"Do you know Hilton Ruiz?"

"Yes. I love his playing."

"I took him all the way back to Fats Waller, and that's what you need to do. You also need some more modern voicings."

The rest of the lesson was a blur.

Mostly, we worked on voicings and harmony.

My great regret is that I didn't ask her to play something for me.

*   *   *

I walked out of her front door grateful but humbled.

I came in to show off my bebop chops, and this woman listened for a few seconds to my virtuoso ramblings and then told me to look backwards!

Nonetheless, heeding her advice was one of the best decisions I could have ever made.

By studying jazz's deeper roots, I was eventually to find a rootedness and strength in my own playing that could not have come any other way.

Sometimes going back is the best way to move forward.

Mary Lou knew the secret. Don't skip steps.

Build a solid foundation for whatever you want to learn.

Skipping steps is rampant these days in just about every area of our lives. Just go to the Web and everybody's trying to sell you the fast and easy way to fame, fortune, love, mastery.

Every field with a relatively low barrier to entry and a potentially lucrative payoff (for example, music, coaching, and entertainment) will attract slick marketers who encourage you to skip steps. Once you buy their course, learn their system, follow their method, you discover it didn't work quite the way they promised.

What they don't tell you is that it's probably not your fault.

They were selling the illusion that you can skip steps to success.

It doesn't work that way.

*   *   *

A young man approached me a couple of months back for music advice. He had been playing the piano for less than a year and was ready, in his own mind, to start writing, marketing, and performing his own music. Yet he could not tell the difference between a major or minor chord. When I asked who and what he listened to, what pianists, what music, he could not name one artist whose music appealed to him that he wanted to model himself after. He was trying to skip steps.

In conversation with a new and talented life coach, I advised her not to stick out her shingle too quickly.

I continued, "If you're training to become a lawyer, doctor, or therapist, you would expect to endure a prolonged internship where you would get to work with many people, for up to 1000 hours or more, under the supervision of skilled mentors, before you were even considered to be granted a license to legally practice your profession."

She was expecting to attract clients who would pay her substantial fees after completing her first couple of weekend workshops. She was trying to skip steps.

*   *   *

Here are a few more examples of skipping steps, all of which I have personally observed in friends, acquaintances, and clients I've known.

The goal is to enjoy a happy, fulfilling marriage, but the couple refuses to handle their individual issues or ask each other the tough questions before they walk down the aisle.

The goal is to launch yourself as an expert, but you base your advice only on your own personal experience without researching and learning enough about your field of expertise.

The goal is to become a professional coach, practitioner, or healer, but you choose to first build a great-looking website, aggressively network, charge high fees, and then wing it, refusing to pay your dues by first mastering the craft or bothering to learn about professional boundaries and ethics.

There is a good reason that so many people attempt to skip steps, particularly in fields related to human wellbeing.

The guardians of the gate in the medical-pharmaceutical-psychological-industrial complex have suppressed and discredited often-valuable innovations that did not offer adequate opportunities for profiteering or that powerfully threatened the status quo.

I have also met many who have really suffered from the misguided and rigid advice of otherwise highly credentialed professionals. Credentials and certifications alone do not lead to real professionalism, deep empathy, or true mastery. But they do, however, indicate a willingness not to skip steps.

So let's not throw the baby out with the bathwater.

Don't buy into a step-skipping, instant-gratification culture.

Whatever steps you skip today, you'll eventually have to go back and deal with tomorrow.

Why not follow Mary Lou Williams's advice?

It's paid off for me.

Don't skip steps.

Thanks, Ms. Williams, for taking me back to basics.

Chapter 12

Milt Jackson's Sage Advice

You become what you think about most of the time.

—EARL NIGHTINGALE

IT WAS THE MORNING AFTER MY SECOND GIG WITH THE MILT Jackson Quartet. On the short flight back to New York from St. Louis, I had the honor of sitting next to "Bags."

I'd performed with Mr. Jackson once before, thanks to Cedar Walton's endorsement, and the St. Louis concert had been a blast—a tour de force of pure unadulterated swing.

It's amazing how much you can learn just by being in the presence of a master. Their very mastery emanates a vibration, an energy that you can connect with and tune into, an unseen power that mysteriously but potently accelerates your own growth and development. That's one reason why apprenticeship continues to be one of the most powerful and practical ways to develop high levels of skill in any domain.

That morning, en route back to LaGuardia International Airport, Mr. Milt Jackson gave me the single most important piece of practical advice I've heard before or since. I don't remember much else that we talked about (I was honestly still very much in awe of the man), but there was one thing he said that I would never forget.

Four simple words that shifted my worldview—and my world—forever.

"Harry, always remember, association brings about assimilation."

Bags was laying down some words of wisdom for a young pianist just getting started in the world of music.

Association brings about assimilation. You become like that (and those) with which you associate. Your friends determine your future. Like attracts like. As above, so below.

Stated in countless ways throughout the centuries, it's even been proven recently in the psychology lab. It's not limited only to behavior; even our emotions and values are literally contagious.

Hang out with overweight friends and you skyrocket your own likelihood of being overweight.

Too many depressed, or alcoholic, or angry, or materialistic friends? You pick up those traits as well.

And of course, the same is true of happiness and life satisfaction. Even the percentage of happy friends your friends have will have a significant impact on your own happiness.

Even our thoughts are prone to this universal law. The more we focus on worry, the more worried we become. On the other hand, as we bring our attention to gratitude, we become happier.

Association brings about assimilation. Dang, Milt. This is heavy stuff.

To get better at anything faster, hang out with people who are better than you. Their influence will rub off, slowly but surely.

To become a better musician, play with people who are better than you.

* * *

I first learned this lesson when I was 15. I started my first summer at Brevard Music Center as an okay sight-reader.

Then I got lucky.

I became friends with the first-chair violinist and the first-chair cellist in Brevard's youth orchestra. They loved chamber music and were looking for a piano player who was willing to read through the trio repertoire. I volunteered. The better pianists were all busy practicing their concerti and recital pieces. I wasn't that good (I was actually there to play baritone horn in the wind ensemble and concert band), but I had lots of free time.

So for seven solid weeks, I spent on average two to three hours a day reading through all of the Mozart, Beethoven, Haydn, and Schubert trios for violin, cello, and piano. The floors of my practice room were piled high with wrong notes, but it didn't matter.

I kept showing up. Night after night. And I got better.

By summer's end, I was a decent sight-reader. Plus, I had a new model of what was possible.

Association brings about assimilation.

The more time and attention I give to anything—a subject, a skill, an emotion, a goal, a spiritual aspiration, a desire—the more I become like that thing, the more I discover about that thing, the more I understand that thing, the more I grow into a living embodiment of that thing.

The entire basis of spiritual practice is to cultivate the

development of certain states and ways of being that ultimately reflect qualities of God.

In fact, my entire personal theology can be captured in six simple words that also reflect this universal principle: God is love; be like God.

Association brings about assimilation.

It's been stated countless times in different ways throughout the ages. You become what you think about most. As above, so below. As within, so without. Your friends determine your future. A thousand ways to say the same thing.

Could these four words contain the ultimate secret to a fulfilling life?

* * *

Bags knew. By that time in his life, he had become a jazz icon, an undisputed master of all things swing. He had also shared the stage with virtually every jazz legend who ever lived.

And to think that I was lucky enough to receive from him this profound gift of generosity, the planting of a seed of wisdom that I could never forget, a seed that would take decades to bloom.

Four words summarizing the most important thing this man had learned that he now chose to pass on to this young'un, who, in that moment, felt like the luckiest man alive.

Association brings about assimilation.

Thanks, Bags. Your groove still lives.

Chapter 13

Nothing I Heard Could Have Prepared Me for This

*If you have something to say of any worth
then people will listen to you.*

—OSCAR PETERSON

I'LL NEVER FORGET THAT SUNDAY EVENING. IT WAS A HOT August night in Brunswick, Georgia, a typical boring weekend night. It was the summer after I had graduated from high school, with a good month to go before I would travel to North Carolina to begin my freshman year at Davidson College.

Might as well watch some TV. Nothing else to do.

So I'm flipping through the four channels—that's right, only four—ABC, NBC, CBS, and PBS—available back in those media Stone Age days.

Let's see. There's *60 Minutes*. No.

How about *The Wonderful World of Disney*? Nope. No Tinker Bell tonight.

Then I turned the channel.

Oh. My. God. What *is* that man doing? Whoa. No way. Wow.

Sunday nights on PBS featured entertaining and educational episodes of *Previn and the Pittsburgh*. André Previn, the dashing and debonair conductor of the Pittsburgh Symphony Orchestra, seemed at the time heir apparent to the orchestral conductor/educator/pop star role premiered by Leonard Bernstein a decade before.

Every week he would guide audiences through the world of classical music, bringing the world's symphonic masterpieces, plus his witty commentary, into homes all across the United States.

But this Sunday night, there was no orchestra on stage.

Just Previn on a barstool, two pianos, and another man. I didn't recognize this fellow, who was built more like a NFL linebacker than a pianist.

But I had never, ever in my life heard anything like the music he was coaxing from the piano with such effortless ease. His head slightly raised, toes tapping to the beat, a gentle smile breaking out across his wide face, Canadian pianist Oscar Peterson was tearing up that piano.

I was transfixed. What was this? His impeccable technique, unrelenting swing, and utter, absolute, and total mastery of the piano astonished me.

I stayed glued to the screen for the next 52 minutes.

* * *

I had never even imagined the piano could be played like this.

Sure, I had some exposure to jazz through my high school

stage band. There were a couple of Erroll Garner and Duke Ellington albums in the house. I'd even made the piano chair in all-state stage band, because I had learned how to read chord symbols years ago when I took organ lessons at Hick's Music Store. (We had a Baldwin OrgaSonic, complete with a built-in rhythm machine, and learning how to pedal the bass part and play chords in the left hand underneath a soaring melody in the right was the core curriculum at my weekly lessons.)

But nothing I had ever seen, heard, or played prepared me for Oscar Peterson.

My jaw dropped, and my eyes grew wide with amazement as I bore witness to the musical miracle unfolding before my eyes.

I didn't know what it was he was doing on that piano. But I did know one thing—I had to find out.

By the time the show was over, I was buzzing with excitement. The next morning, I got up bright and early to visit the two record stores in town.

"Do you have any albums by Oscar Peterson?"

"Oscar who? Sorry."

I should have known better. After all, this was Brunswick, Georgia, and I was much more likely to find Liberace, Dolly Parton, or the Ohio Players' latest album than anything remotely resembling jazz.

These were the pre-Amazon, pre-MP3 player, pre-download days. I would have to somehow find or order a round piece of vinyl before I could hear this man play again.

Thoroughly disappointed, I left the second record shop.

Then I had a hunch.

The local Goodwill store was just two blocks away. There was a stack of old albums and 78s over on the bottom shelf near the back wall, where I regularly picked up classical LPs for a dollar apiece. I drove to the store, rushed to the stack, and started to sort through the two-foot tall pile of albums.

About three quarters of the way through, I found it.

Verve Records. *The Oscar Peterson Trio. Live From Chicago.* I couldn't believe my good fortune.

Ten minutes later, I was back home in my bedroom, filled with excited anticipation. I put the album on my Radio Shack turntable and gently lowered the stylus.

For the next three days, I listened to Oscar, Ray Brown, and Ed Thigpen holding jazz court in Chicago. I could not stop listening. Even when I would get called away to eat lunch or dinner, the sound of jazz in the background consumed my attention.

To this day, I can replay the entire album in my mind: from the very first note, the intro to "I've Never Been in Love Before," to the deep groove of "Sometimes I'm Happy," to the locked hands refrain of "Chicago," to the delicate and tender "In the Wee Small Hours of the Morning," and the riotous and virtuosic "Billy Boy."

Every single song opened a door to a new musical universe for me.

I knew that day that I had to commit myself to learning everything I could about this new world of jazz. Thirty-eight years later, I am still learning.

Thank you, Oscar. And thanks, André, for the introduction.

Chapter 14

The Best Class Ever

You wish to rise? Begin by descending. You plan a tower that
will pierce the clouds? Lay first the foundation of humility.

—SAINT AUGUSTINE

I COULDN'T BELIEVE IT.

D-?

I got a D-?

On my very first English paper. Of my very first quarter. Of
my very first year of college.

This was definitely not a good sign.

There were so many red marks on my paper that I could
hardly see the typewritten words underneath.

And his handwriting was so tiny and precise. Anal. That's
what it was. Anal.

I could feel his rigid judgement of my every word reeking
from the page. And this class was a requirement. No way out
of this one.

How dare he?

I was a smart guy.

I was fourth in my graduating class of over four hundred.

Plus, I already knew how to write.

I'd always received As in English (even that one time in eighth grade when Mrs. Frazier gave me an A in achievement and a B in effort because she was annoyed that I could do so well without even trying).

But here I was, a lowly freshman at prestigious Davidson College, around all these equally smart kids, staring at the bright red D- on the top of my paper.

Okay, Dr. Randy Nelson, you want to give me a D-? I felt a mixture of shock and indignation. I looked around at my classmates. All seemed to be in a similar state of disbelief.

Barbara, how did you do? I got an F. Really? How about you, Jim? F. Sarah? F.

My quick poll of peers indicated universal misery.

Within moments, it dawned on me.

I had received the only passing grade.

As much as the evil Dr. Nelson sought to annihilate my self-esteem, he could not flunk me as he did everyone else.

No, sucker.

I *passed!* The only passing grade in class—on my first essay during the first quarter of my first year in college.

Suddenly I didn't feel so terrible.

Of course, I had a lot of work to do, and subsequent weeks of Dr. Nelson's class forced me to pay closer attention to my writing and my thinking than I had ever dreamed possible.

Now I carry that D- as a badge of honor.

As I look back, I see how those 10 weeks in Dr. Nelson's class provided the single most valuable and life-transforming experience of my college career.

I still remember his mantra—fewer words, more ideas.

I can still see his tiny, impeccably neat (still anal) red writing all over my papers, and remember how I would labor for hours writing and rewriting and editing and refining until finally, I had created something that (I hoped) was worthy for Dr. Nelson to read.

I can still feel the pride I felt when I ultimately earned an A in English composition—the most well-deserved A in my entire academic career.

My biggest lessons from Dr. Nelson:

First drafts always stink; just get the words on paper. Edit fiercely, mercilessly. Then do it again.

Trim the fat. Don't stop until your words powerfully express your best and clearest thinking.

And don't be afraid to fail. Failure's only an opportunity to learn, adapt, and start anew.

Best class I ever took.

Best advice I ever received.

Best D- I ever earned.

Thank you, Dr. Nelson.

Your red pen still lights up my life.

P.S. I wrote Dr. Nelson a thank-you email the same day I completed this chapter. Here it is.

6.27.2015

Dear Dr. Nelson,

You might remember our brief conversation about a decade ago when I visited Davidson to present a concert.

I was enrolled in your English composition class during the first quarter of my first year of college. It was 1977, which I believe was also your first year teaching.

I found you incredibly intimidating, particularly once you

graded and returned my very first assignment. Not only was the paper filled with your distinctive commentary in your signature tiny red print, but on the top of the page, your graded assessment of my linguistic brilliance cut me to the core.

D-.

Thanks a lot, Doc.

I was instantly cast into an inconsolable darkness, until I looked around.

Every one of my classmates received an F. I actually had earned the highest grade in my class.

Perhaps I was less ignorant than I thought. Maybe you pitied me and chose to grant me a smidgen of mercy.

Or maybe I had done a few things right, and could learn a great deal from this red-pen-obsessed newly minded hotshot PhD who was as new to this campus as I was.

Thank you, Dr. Randy Nelson!

Even now, in 2015, at the ripe young age of 55, I continue to see your class as a significant turning point in my academic and personal life.

As I find myself writing more and more (I'm working on three nonfiction books now—two textbooks and one spiritual/musical memoir), I continue to return to the basic principles you so generously and emphatically shared those 36 years ago.

Your mantra, "fewer words, more ideas," remains with me.

Every word I write carries the imprint of your guidance.

Your influence now touches the lives of all I am privileged to serve.

Thank you.

All the best,

Harry Pickens

Davidson class of 1981

PART IV

In Tune with Imagination

CREATING FROM WITHIN

Music from the Inside Out

Imagination is the beginning of creation.
You imagine what you desire; you will what you imagine;
and at last you create what you will.
—GEORGE BERNARD SHAW

I LOVED THE BREVARD WIND ENSEMBLE.

Our conductor, Jamie Hafner, was not only smart and funny, he was a tuba player. Since my primary instrument was euphonium (the tuba's little brother), we already had a lot in common.

I was also lucky enough to have private lessons with Mr. Hafner.

It was inspiring to play in an ensemble with such high musical standards, such amazing musicians, and to have the positive pressure of doing a brand new concert every single week.

And we took on hard music—Tchaikovsky's *Symphony No. 4*, "Procession of the Nobles," "Aegean Festival Overture," "Lincolnshire Posy," and *Persichetti Symphony for Band*. I still have the cassette tapes from that magical summer of 1975 and to this day, I am astounded by how good we sounded.

This particular morning, Mr. Hafner did something that I'd never experienced before. He used a stunningly simple technique to get us in synch with the spirit, pulse, and mood of the music.

We were rehearsing the *William Byrd Suite*, a straightforward band arrangement of several of Renaissance composer Byrd's keyboard works. Since each part of the suite was a dance, creating a vital yet buoyant rhythmic pulse was incredibly important.

And we weren't getting it. Our galliard was sluggish, like we were dancing in knee-deep mud. So Hafner stopped us.

"All right. This is a dance. We need more dance in the music. I want you to put your instruments down and sing your parts. Sing on the syllable 'ta.'"

Sing? We were a band, not a chorus. Why should we sing the parts? We're having enough trouble trying to play.

I could feel a wave of resistance go through the entire ensemble. This was weird.

Despite my inner objections, I had little choice. He was the boss, and his advice had taken us to such musical heights that I would have done absolutely anything this man requested.

So, in spite of our collective shyness, we began to sing.

We sang the passage over and over again, until our voices reflected the exact synthesis of rhythmic intensity, buoyant energy, and clear phrasing that Hafner was seeking.

"Okay, now play."

I would not have believed such a transformation was possible if I had not been there to hear it with my very own ears.

Our playing was totally different. The galliard felt like a dance now. We bounced and danced, the pulse now alive in our bodies and hearts, easily and effortlessly translating through our instruments.

That day planted a seed of musical insight for me that would continue to grow and blossom for the rest of my life.

*   *   *

Fast-forward 40 years.

It's late June 2015, and I'm coaching a wind quintet of talented high schoolers. I have 15 to 20 minutes to work with them, then I go on to the next group, so I need to help them get results fast.

We're at the Kentucky Governor's School for the Arts, and these enterprising youngsters are tackling the polka from Shostakovich's *Golden Age* ballet.

I listen to them play through the piece one time.

Then we get to work.

"So on a zero-to-ten scale, zero lousy and ten awesome, what number would you give that performance?"

"I'd give it a six."

"Five point five."

"Six."

"Six."

"Six or six and a half."

"Okay, about a six. And if there was one thing you could do that would immediately take it up to an eight or nine, what would that be?"

"Dynamics."

"Expression."

"Better rhythm."

"I'd say dynamics."

"Me, too. Dynamics."

"Great. Your answers show that you really are paying attention to the important things—the musicality of it all."

"So we're off to a good start. I have a question. If this music was a soundtrack for a movie, what do you suppose you would see on the screen?"

"Clowns."

"Charlie Chaplin."

"Something funny."

"People dancing."

"Happy people."

"Thank you. Those are all great ideas. I wonder if, this time when you play the piece, you could play it as though you were accompanying that movie live. And I'd love to see some part of your bodies moving with the pulse—also could be a tapping toe or your left elbow. Just make sure your body is expressing the beat in some way."

(Take 2)

"That was much better. Now let's add even more expression to it. This time, instead of playing, let's sing the parts. Don't worry too much about the pitches, we're going for a buoyant spirit and precise rhythm and dynamics. One, two, ready, begin!"

(Singing)

"Much, much better. Now let's add one more thing. This time, sing your parts on the syllables ho, ha, or hee. Make it laughing music." (They giggle).

"And fill the room with joy and humor while you imagine those clowns dancing on the screen."

(Singing on ho, ha, and hee)

"That was so much better. What did you notice?"

"It was more fun."

"Our dynamics and expression improved a lot."

"It just felt better—bouncier."

"Exactly. So we're going to do this a couple more times, because you're starting to catch the spirit of the piece now. I want you to pantomime, like you're actually playing your instruments, and finger along, while you sing. No playing just yet, and as you pantomime, remember the feeling and dancing and clowns and dynamics and all the rest. You're doing really well."

(Singing and pantomiming)

"Bingo! That was great. Now let's play it."

(Take 3)

This time, the Shostakovich quintet came to life.

And we only played the passages a total of three times in just 20 minutes, yet the musicianship and expression and dynamics and spirit of the music improved exponentially.

*   *   *

I've seen this happen with hundreds of musicians, from soloists to chamber ensembles, to bands, orchestras, and jazz bands over the past 40 years.

Sing the parts until the musical expression is just right. Then it's simply a matter of translating this inwardly sensed ideal sound through the instrument.

Thanks, Mr. Hafner.

I explain it to students this way.

"If your name is Sabrina and you misspell your name Sabrinea when you type it into a computer, then print out a copy, what do you see on the printed page?"

"The misspelled name."

"If you have a glitch in your word processing software or your spell-check program and it consistently misspells your name, what do you see on the printout?"

"The misspelled name."

"As within, so without. If there's a glitch in the program, there's going to be a glitch in the printout. The same is true with music. Our internal experience of the phrase, the tone, the rhythm, the articulation, is what determines the outer expression. If the image in our imagination is unclear, sloppy, imprecise, we can't help but send a signal to our body to replicate that flawed image. On the other hand, once we correct the internal image, then we are much more likely to replicate that inner ideal in our playing and singing."

* * *

Decades of research on visualization and mental rehearsal in both the athletic and performance domains demonstrates the power of refining and cultivating a vivid and multi-sensory internal image of the desired result.

The clearer, better, more precise the inner image, the better the outer performance.

Fix the software and the printout will take care of itself.

That's the lesson that Mr. Hafner was teaching us that balmy summer morning. It's so easy to get stuck on the page, to buy into the hallucination that the notes are the music.

When we return to our voices as a direct expression of what's on the inside, we reconnect with the essence of music, which is always invisible, intangible, pure sonic expression.

Feel the pulse and make the music from the inside out. Sing the parts until every detail is precisely like you want it—the shape and articulation of each phrase, the rhythmic precision, the dynamic contrasts, the balance and blend, the emotional tone—fix it on the inside first, without the complication of an external instrument.

Then play, and you will begin to feel and hear the music, not just the notes.

Since then, multiple studies have validated the use of mental rehearsal in improving every imaginable skill, from tennis to public speaking to musical performance.

The connection between the invisible reality of thought and the visible reality of manifestation has also been a principle explored by many of the great philosophers, sages, and mystics throughout human history.

"As a man thinketh in his heart, so is he."

"Thoughts are things."

"We become what we think about."

"As above, so below—as within, so without."

Ancient wisdom and modern science concur. Success begins on the inside.

Thanks, Jamie Hafner, for helping us learn to imagine—and sing—our way to free musical expression.

Chapter 16

What You See is What You Get

I would visualize things coming to me. It would just
make me feel better. Visualization works if you work hard.
That's the thing. You can't just visualize and go eat a sandwich.

—JIM CARREY

IT'S AROUND TWO P.M. ON SATURDAY, MAY 19, 2013. I'M standing backstage at the KFC Yum! Center in downtown Louisville, waiting to go on. Fifteen thousand people have been here for most of the day.

In the next 30 minutes, I will be playing for them all—including His Holiness the Dalai Lama, who is sitting fewer than 20 feet away.

I close my eyes and imagine a movie screen in front of me. On that screen, I begin to watch myself, in my imagination, walk onto the stage, face the crowd, take a bow, introduce my piece, sit at the piano, play with total focus and expression, acknowledge the thunderous applause, bow to the Dalai Lama, and return backstage.

Next, I enter into the movie in my imagination, so that now I can feel it as real throughout my body. This scene becomes so vivid that, although I don't actually see a bright inner image, nonetheless I get the feeling as though I am actually there. I repeat this process continually, returning over and over to my mental movie, both observing and feeling it from the inside out.

By the time I am actually called to the stage, I've already been there (in my mind, heart and IVR, my inner virtual reality) at least a dozen times this afternoon and a few dozen more times over the previous few days.

The actual performance feels like déjà vu.

I've been here before. Actually, a few thousand times over the past few decades.

Here's what I mean.

I first discovered the astonishing power of mental rehearsal nearly 40 years ago.

At the time, my stage fright was sometimes debilitating. I experienced absolutely no stage fright when I played in a group or when performing on the baritone horn in band or wind ensemble, but there was something about being all alone on stage that just freaked me out.

Whenever I had a solo piano performance, I would stop sleeping through the night about a week in advance. A few days later, I could count on at least a few of my meals coming back up the way they went down. A day or two before the performance, I would wake up with my heart racing at 120 to 140 beats per minute.

Not good signs for an aspiring professional musician!

I knew I had to do something to get myself together, or else I could kiss my dreams goodbye. One of the first things I researched was hypnosis. By learning to get myself into a state of deep relaxation, and then vividly imagining the state

I wanted to be in, I could, over time, recondition my mind and body to access that state at will.

I also explored sports psychology, NLP (neuro-linguistic programming, a methodology for modeling and replicating excellence in any field), cognitive therapy, brain research, autogenic training, Silva Mind Control, and anything else I could put my hands on that could help me get beyond this chronic performance anxiety.

My most important discovery?

I could, through consistent, diligent practice, eventually reprogram my old habitual fear responses. I could change my outer reality by changing how I experienced my inner reality. I could actually create a new "neural highway" in my brain that would allow me to perform more and more consistently towards the top range of my abilities.

Today, my own performance-related anxiety is a thing of the past.

My only experience when performing for anyone now is a deep joy and delight in having the opportunity to share the gift of music.

Now I help others transform stage fright into rock-solid confidence much more easily and quickly than I ever could have imagined, often accomplishing in an hour or two that which took me many months to do.

The next time you have a performance of any kind on the horizon, just take the time to see, hear, feel, sense, and imagine already being the performer—and person—you most desire to become. You might just amaze yourself.

Chapter 17

Harvesting Positive Musical Moments

Memories are the key not to the past, but to the future.
—CORRIE TEN BOOM

A DREAM COME TRUE.

Summer 1986. Mount Fuji, Japan. I was about to begin our trio set.

Ralph Peterson, Kenny Davis, and I were playing the music of Bud Powell.

We breezed through Bud's intricate yet melodious tunes in front of the ten thousand fans. "Parisian Thoroughfare." "Un Poco Loco." "Blue Pearl." We were confident. Fierce. Inspired. Swinging.

And that standing ovation?

We earned it.

This was my third day at the Mount Fuji Jazz Festival, where I had the honor of performing and hanging out with a who's who of jazz. Johnny Griffin. Freddie Hubbard. Milt Jackson. Art Blakey. Bobby Hutcherson. Herbie Hancock. Billy Higgins. Ron Carter.

I felt right at home, confident in my abilities and performing at my best.

What a journey it had been.

* * *

Just a few short years earlier, the very idea of ever performing with such confidence, passion, joy, and ease, especially in the presence of these master musicians, would have been a total pipe dream for me.

In fact, nearly every time I sat down to play, the same self-sabotaging habits would return.

Image after image of my very worst performance moments would flash through my mind.

Like the time I lost my place in the changes and forced the entire quartet to stop and start over again.

Or the time during my high school piano recital when I reached over to turn the page of the sheet music and it fell off the piano, and I stumbled through the rest of the piece, constantly on the verge of panic.

Or perhaps that disdainful look the singer gave me when she realized I couldn't transpose up a minor third to her key at sight.

Or that audition where I kept speeding up until I ended the piece literally twice as fast as I began it.

Then the critical voice would pipe in. You know the one.

The voice of doom.

I know I'm going to mess up. I just wonder how soon it'll happen. I hope I don't screw up again. I should have practiced this a lot more. Uh oh, here comes that part I always miss. I bet they think this is really bad. Oops. I can't believe _____ is here listening to me and I am playing this badly.

Now add the physical symptoms. Cold clammy hands. Racing heartbeat. Beads of sweat.

No wonder I rarely performed at my best.

My mind was full to the brim with my private personal musical horror movies guaranteed to end in disaster.

Until the day everything began to change.

I walked into a used bookstore just a few blocks from Rutgers' New Brunswick campus. My eyes fell on a paperback with a white, pink, and black cover, a funny title, and a 50-cent price tag.

It was Maxwell Maltz's *Psycho-Cybernetics*.

This classic self-help tome was written by a plastic surgeon who noticed his patients didn't feel any better on the inside even after they got the new nose, or bigger (or smaller) breasts, or tucked tummy.

He pondered why the outer change didn't have the desired impact.

What he discovered was simple yet profound.

Our brain has an automatic goal-seeking (cybernetic) mechanism that helps us move in the direction of the mental images that dominate our minds. To change our results, we must first transform these inner images.

If we inwardly see failure, we will be more likely to act in ways that all but guarantee failure. On the other hand, inward images of success will tend to lead us towards the feelings and actions that make success more likely.

Maltz realized that although his patients changed on the outside, their corresponding mental images had not yet transformed. Until this occurred, they would never be satisfied with their outer appearance, no matter how much external perfection they attained.

I realized that my own brain's automatic mechanism was set up to give me more of what I didn't want. More performance anxiety. More fear. More failure. I needed to somehow cultivate more positive and empowering images to populate my mental village.

So I began two practices that were to forever change my experience of performing, and ultimately help me transform stage fright into confidence.

First, I learned to create mental movies wherein I would watch myself performing at my best.

I would simply close my eyes, imagine a movie screen, and then watch and hear myself on the screen performing with total confidence, fluency, and ease. Next, I would step into the movie in my imagination and feel what it felt like to perform well.

I would repeat this mental imagery several times each day, making this an important aspect of my practice routine.

The second practice that transformed my performance experience was what I call positivity harvesting.

I started collecting positive musical memories. Every time I would actually feel good and play well, either when practicing or performing, I would make a brief note of the experience in my journal.

Over the next ten years, I chronicled nearly a thousand of these positive musical moments. I eventually labeled them my musical moments of grace—times when the music would flow through me, when body, mind, and spirit were aligned and fully available to the musical impulse, when I felt inwardly connected to the magic and power of whatever emotion I wanted to express.

For over a year, my end-of-the-day ritual was the same.

I would go through my list, choose four or five of these

positive musical moments, and remember each as vividly as I could. At first it was hard to get the feeling back. Sometimes it would take me several minutes to fully recapture.

But over time, this mental muscle grew stronger and stronger. Eventually I reached a point where I could access the feeling of these memories almost instantly.

Then, once I could recall the feeling vividly, the next step was to project this feeling forward into my upcoming performance.

I would now imagine myself sometime in the future, fully experiencing the positive state I had just recalled.

In the weeks preceding the Mount Fuji Festival, I harvested many positive musical moments of grace, recalling and amplifying the feelings, and then projecting them forward as I imagined the upcoming performance. By the time I walked on stage, my mind was so filled with empowering thoughts, feelings, and images, that confident performance was nearly inevitable.

When have you experienced musical moments of grace?

Begin paying attention when they occur. Record them in a journal or app, practice consciously recalling them, amplifying the feeling, and then projecting that feeling forward as you imagine yourself performing with confidence and ease.

The transformation from anxiety-ridden performance to rock-solid confidence can begin when you simply harvest one positive memory at a time.

Chapter 18

I'll Never Play the Piano Again (She Said)

The only true voyage of discovery ... would be
not to visit strange lands but to possess other eyes ...
—MARCEL PROUST

KELLY CAME JUST TO BE WITH HER BOYFRIEND.

I had invited everyone to identify their instrument or voice type. I wanted to learn a bit more about who was in the room before we jumped into exploring strategies for more effective practice.

"So, Kelly, you don't play or sing?"

"Well, I used to play the piano—a long time ago. But not anymore."

She hadn't touched it in 10 years. Convinced she would never play again.

"What brought you here to the workshop?"

"He asked me to come."

"Okay, great. Well, welcome. So, may I ask you a question?"

"Sure."

"I'm curious why you don't play anymore. Do you not enjoy it?"

"Oh, no. I love the piano. I love music. I just can't play anymore."

"Did something happen to your hands?"

"No. I just . . . can't."

"Well, I'm happy you're here."

*   *   *

After the workshop, her boyfriend came up to thank me. What he'd learned about practice had changed a lot for him.

I acknowledged his appreciation, then asked about his girlfriend. "So, what's up that she doesn't play piano anymore?"

"It's sort of a long story. She had a couple of bad experiences with a teacher and a recital."

Hmm. I thought that might be the case.

I called her over.

"Kelly, I have a question for you. I know you don't play anymore, but I'm curious. If you could be totally free of the pain of your past experiences, and truly enjoy playing again, would you want to?"

"Oh my gosh! Of course, I would. I just stopped because of what happened."

"All right. I'm only here on campus until lunch tomorrow. If you two have the time, I'd be happy to spend an hour with you. I think together there is a chance we can heal some of this old pain and get you playing again. Would you be willing to give it a shot?"

"Absolutely."

"Let's meet at 10 in the morning. Do you have a place we can go that will be quiet and undisturbed for an hour?"

"Sure. We could go to the science building. I have a key to the lab, and nobody is there on Saturday morning."

"Great. See you there."

* * *

The next day, they both showed up at the guesthouse where I was staying during my two-day campus visit. We walked across campus to the lab and got to work.

"Okay, Kelly, I don't need to know the story of what happened to you, unless you want to share it. What I've discovered is that sometimes when people have something happen to them that is really painful emotionally, the experience gets stored in their brain in a particular way that keeps them stuck. They are not able to move beyond that experience without the emotional pain continually coming back. So they just avoid whatever triggers the pain. That's how phobias happen."

"That's exactly why I can't play the piano.

"Here's the story. When I was 10, I had a piano recital. I chose the piece I was going to play, but my teacher thought it was too hard for me. Well, maybe she was right; after all, I was only 10 at the time.

"The day of the recital came around. It was my turn to play.

"Everything started out okay, but midway through my piece, I went blank. I could not remember the next part. I started again from the beginning, and went blank again in the same place.

"I quickly took a bow and ran back to my seat in the audience, totally humiliated. Then, after the recital, my teacher yelled at me. 'I told you, Kelly! You should have chosen something easier! Now you've embarrassed me and yourself as well!'

"I was so upset. Humiliated. Afraid. Ashamed. She was so mad. Anyhow, that's what happened. I refused to go back to piano lessons after that and haven't been able to touch a piano since."

"Wow. Thanks for sharing that story. I can really understand why you made the choices you've made. So we're going to free you from the pain of those memories, and see if your desire to play comes back, okay?"

"Sure. Do you really think it's possible?"

"Well, we're going to find out."

So we got to work.

* * *

I had been intensively studying several new techniques—grounded in brain research—that help people quickly heal their emotions and rewire their brains for less stress, greater resilience, and more joy and fulfillment.

I'd used some of the more promising of these methods to help let go of my own fears, resentments, and worries. I'd also been helping my students transform performance fears into rock-solid confidence, so I was quite certain I could help Kelly.

I began by showing her how to change the inner cinematic features of the way she stored and replayed her experiences.

At first, every time she thought of the recital, she found herself in the middle of a bright, loud, colorful 3D movie, looking out at the piano, her angry teacher, and the audience through her own eyes.

We shifted each relevant, fully associated memory to a dim, black-and-white snapshot that she placed very far away. This immediately shifted her feelings about the memory.

I also had her use meridian tapping (derived from Emotional Freedom Technique) to completely neutralize the emotional discomfort she associated with these experiences.

We needed to address several specific incidents, each of which carried a high emotional charge: the memory slip moment, running back to her seat in tears, the teacher's yelling, and the argument with her mother about her refusal to return to piano lessons. Once she completely cleared each memory and she could go back and recall each mental scenario with zero negative emotional charge, I asked her how she felt about playing the piano again.

She took a moment to reflect, and said, "I think I could."

"Great. Let's walk back over to the guesthouse, where there's a piano in the lounge, and find out. You up for that?"

"Sure."

*   *   *

On our way back across campus, I asked about her favorite songs and her most fun memories of the piano, and she was able to talk freely about these topics with no signs of distress.

We arrived at the guesthouse, she walked to the piano, sat down, and began playing Beethoven's "Für Elise," which had been her favorite song to play before the recital calamity occurred.

She played beautifully, with sensitive phrasing, and was a bit incredulous afterward.

"I'm actually playing the piano! And it doesn't feel bad. I don't feel like something's wrong with me!"

She continued to play a few more songs that she remembered from her earlier studies.

"Thank you so much."

"You're welcome."

The last I heard from her, she is still playing and enjoying music, once again having fun at the piano.

Kelly's story demonstrates once more the fact that we are living in an incredibly exciting time, a time of unprecedented promise and potential for personal and collective transformation.

We now have access to practical, proven tools and techniques that can help anyone release the pain of the past, experience greater inner harmony in the present, and consciously create a better future.

I am excited to share these tools for thriving with as many people as I can.

To learn more about the tools I used to help Kelly, go to www.thrivingnow.com, www.havening.org, and www. nlpcomprehensive.com.

PART V

In Tune with Discipline

DOING EVERY DAY

Chapter 19

Bud Powell, the Pitch Pipe, and Me

A little more persistence, a little more effort, and what seemed hopeless failure may turn to glorious success.

—ELBERT HUBBARD

IT'S TWO O'CLOCK ON A HUMID SATURDAY AFTERNOON IN September.

I sit on the side of my bed in the tiny room I'm renting in East Orange, New Jersey, pitch pipe in hand. On my left, resting on the bed, lies a Radio Shack portable cassette recorder. Spread across the bed on my right is a pile of music manuscript paper.

I press the play button. Out of the tiny (and tinny) speaker comes measure 11 of Bud Powell's first chorus on "Sonny Side" (from the Prestige 1724 LP, recorded with Sonny Stitt in 1949). I am determined that I will finish transcribing this solo today. I've been at it since around eight thirty this morning.

With my cassette player and pitch pipe, I have to go slowly. Catch a note or two. Stop the cassette. Find the note on the pitch pipe. Write it down. Rewind just a tiny bit. Repeat.

This will sound totally bizarre to those reading this who grew up in the digital era. What I'm describing happened in

1979, before email, digital recorders, slow-it-down software, and electronic tuners. Truly the Stone Age compared to the early 21st century.

It took me pretty much all day—from around nine in the morning until about seven that night—to write down a single chorus of Bud playing over the "I Got Rhythm" changes of this tune.

I didn't care how long it would take, because something in me just knew that doing this (transcribing the solos of my musical role models) was going to help me to build the musical and auditory "muscles" I so desperately needed if I was ever going to be able to play the way I wanted to play.

That week, once I got back to the Rutgers' New Brunswick campus, I practiced and learned these 32 measures by heart. I still recall parts of the solo 36 years later.

But this was just the beginning. Every single weekend of that entire school year, from September 1979 to April 1980, my Saturdays were devoted to transcribing solos with my cassette recorder and pitch pipe.

After a couple of months, I started to get the hang of it. By midwinter, I only needed a couple of hours to accomplish what used to take me an entire day. By the spring, I could transcribe one full chorus in about an hour (it took me 10 hours when I first started), a 1000 percent improvement in efficiency over a nine-month period.

The point of the story?

It's this: everything takes longer and feels awkward and frustrating when you're just starting out. That's par for the course when you're a beginner.

Don't let that reality discourage you. The greatest masters in any and every field were not proficient at the beginning. Mastery happens over time, with sustained effort, good coaching and guidance, and lots of grit.

That thing that feels nearly impossible today? A few months from now, you'll look back with astonishment as you realize how far you've come.

Chapter 20

Don't Just Tell Me I'm Talented

Talent is cheaper than table salt.
What separates the talented individual from
the successful one is a lot of hard work.

—STEPHEN KING

SHE MEANT WELL.

After all, she was a little old lady who was deeply touched by my performance. I keep having to remind myself that she meant well, because that reminder muffles the rage that I felt when I first heard her say those words. I know, rage is a strong word. I'll explain in a minute.

Don't get me wrong. I do the best I can to simply and sincerely acknowledge and appreciate anyone's positive response to my work.

But this phrase—"You're so talented"—really bugs me.

Here's why.

Whenever we witness high levels of human excellence, the tendency is to ascribe it to "talent," natural ability, some kind of innate gift that the person simply received and then is able to express.

No doubt, people do have natural, even exceptional abilities and talents that often show up in early childhood.

No question, learning to soar with our strengths and our innate "superpowers" allows us to live more powerfully with less stress and more joy and fulfillment.

Here's my issue with overuse of the "T word."

The paradox of mastery is this: *the higher the level of mastery, the more effortless it appears, and, the more effort it conceals.*

That is, when someone is really good at something, it often appears effortless. At the same time, you can rest assured that this apparent effortlessness conceals massive amounts of hard work, diligence, and sacrifice.

Simply telling someone "You're so talented" can deny, denigrate, and diminish the often-astonishing level of hard work, grit, tenacity, sheer stubbornness, and discipline required for high levels of mastery in any area.

In fact, this kind of praise (psychologists call this person praise) implies a permanent state, unchangeable by effort. Person praise reinforces a fixed mindset, a habit of thinking in which we impose limits on our capacity to learn, grow, and thrive.

According to research, person praise actually diminishes self-efficacy, agency, and self-esteem over time, because it implies we have minimal personal capacity to change (this is just who we are) and it encourages us to look outside ourselves for approval and validation.

Process praise, which focuses on the character traits and behaviors expressed in order to create a desired result ("I can see you really worked hard on that" or "I really appreciate your persistence") tends to encourage a growth mindset, a habit of thinking that leads to higher levels of self-efficacy, agency, and accomplishment.

The little old lady followed up her "You're so talented" with a question.

"So, did you actually study music, or did you just pick it up on your own?"

Ouch.

For me, this statement "You are so talented," can feel like a smack in the face that says, "What you've accomplished was given to you. You didn't really have to work for it. This skill that you express actually has very little to do with you—your character, your effort, your sacrifice. How lucky you are to have been given something that you didn't even have to earn."

It happened another time with a one-on-one coaching client. He meant well. He was powerfully impacted by our work together, and he told me "You're really talented at this."

Subsequent comments indicated that he perceived, because my work with him appeared to be effortless, that I had put minimal effort into developing the skills that facilitated his healing a pattern of thought, feeling, and behavior that had burdened him for literally decades. He had already invested many thousands of dollars and hundreds of hours in sincere, but ultimately futile attempts, to address it.

The client was so astonished that I could help him with something he had struggled with for so long that the results we achieved simply had to be a result of my "talent."

It couldn't possibly be related to the tens of thousands of hours of study and investigation and training and practice in a dozen different personal change modalities; the seven hundred books in my personal library in the domains of psychology, spiritual development, neurobiology, linguistics, and more; the two thousand-plus hours invested working one-on-one with hundreds of students and clients; or my thirty-nine years of nonstop obsession with learning everything I could about how to help people transform.

Nope.

It's all just a matter of talent.

Obviously, I'm not implying that talent doesn't exist. Of course it does.

Nor do I believe every person is born with the same degree of innate potential in every subject or domain.

In 30-plus years as a teacher, I've encountered hundreds if not thousands of truly gifted and talented young people whose propensity for music, science, art, theater, sports, leadership, and more were crystal clear at a very young age.

But propensity does not become proficiency without work—work that often requires hundreds if not thousands of hours.

Even the brilliant demonstrations of Tim Ferris and others that we can learn demanding new skills in as little as a week still require herculean focus, effort, and drive.

We see the breathtaking dance performance. We don't see the physical pain endured day after day; the injuries, the countless times this person woke up tired, exhausted, having zero—absolutely zero—desire to go to the gym or the practice studio—and they did it anyway.

We hear the spellbinding speech. We don't experience the first, second, or third drafts; the years of observing and modeling masters of the craft; the hours of painstaking rehearsal; the dozens (or hundreds) of lousy speeches that preceded this one, each a golden opportunity to do—and fail—and learn—and do again.

Talent might get you started on the road to mastery.

But tenacity, sacrifice, dedication, grit, good role models, courage, coaching, consistency, and a solid work ethic keep you going.

So the next time you witness an outstanding display of human excellence, if you are inspired to say anything at all, how about something like this?

"Thank you. Thank you for your diligence, for your discipline, for your dedication. I can see that you have sacrificed a great deal in order to transform your innate ability into such a high level of mastery. Thanks for sharing it with us."

Just don't stop at "You're so talented."

Please.

Chapter 21

Crossing the Creativity Finish Line

*How you start is important, but it is how you finish
that counts. In the race for success, speed is less important
than stamina. The sticker outlasts the sprinter.*

—B. C. FORBES

"I JUST DON'T FINISH THINGS."

She sat in the very front row.

This was the opening session of GSA—Governor's School for
the Arts—and I had just invited the 256 young people there to
reflect on the one thing they most wanted to learn, discover, or
change over the next three weeks.

She continued. "I start a short story, but halfway through it,
I get bored. So then I start another one. And I end up with all
these unfinished stories. I don't want to keep going this way. If
I could just learn to finish, it would change everything."

I used to struggle with finishing things, too.

In fact, I have entire journals and digital folders full of "song seeds," workshop ideas, project possibilities—none of which have ever seen the light of day in the real world.

On the other hand, for the last several years, I have been more and more consistent about finishing what I start.

I've written one musical, composed dozens of original choral works, written more than one hundred poems, developed and presented five college courses and more than 50 workshops and keynote addresses nationwide. I've also earned six certifications in innovative approaches to mind-body healing, devoted two thousand hours to serving my individual clients, am editing a three-hundred-page oral history chronicling my mother's life, and am currently writing several books, for which I produce an average of two thousand words a day, every day.

So I've learned a lot about finishing.

It wasn't always that way.

For easily the first four decades of my life, I finished only a tiny fraction of what I started.

It was only after I faced a prolonged illness that I truly discovered the secret that now allows me to drive to completion and finish something practically every day.

I was sick off and on for a full 10 years. A combination of toxic mold poisoning, post-concussive trauma, and adrenal exhaustion resulted in prolonged fatigue, significant weight loss, and a diminished will to do much more than survive.

What I hated most about that period of my life (besides feeling miserable) was my inability to follow through on my commitments. I would promise a friend that we would get together to share a meal or take a walk, and when the time came, would end up postponing the visit because I was too tired or ill to follow through.

At the same time, even during this period, when a good

day meant having two or three hours of consistent energy and focus, I found a way to get a lot done.

In fact, when I look back now at what I accomplished, and remember how sick I really was, I am astounded. I kept moving, kept learning, kept creating, kept delivering, even in the face of a struggling body and often melancholy mood.

How did I do that? There are two principles in my personal "finish fast formula."

The first I learned from author Dorothea Brande in her 1936 book, *Wake Up and Live*.

Brande began with her own story. Up until her life-transforming discovery at around the age of 40, she produced very little—an average of two works (short stories, articles, book reviews) per year. In the two years after discovering her "secret," she produced nearly one hundred works, including three books and 24 articles.

The single sentence that allowed her to skyrocket her own creativity—and her ability to finish one project and then move on to the next was this one: Act as though it were impossible to fail.

Act as though it were impossible to fail.

My error in my earlier years was in starting with a lackadaisical attitude. *Maybe this will work out, but maybe it won't. Maybe this will be successful, but it probably won't, so I won't throw my whole self into it.*

Sometimes I felt my endeavors would be successful, and sometimes I didn't. Guess which things tended to get finished?

Around this same time, I also ran across a quote by a man who consistently got things done: author, educator, orator, and activist Booker T. Washington. He wrote: I have begun everything with the idea that I could succeed.

After reading Brande's book, I expanded her basic instruction and began to use the same process for every project that I had used for years to prepare for musical performances.

I would take just a few minutes and imagine myself successful. Not only imagining the end goal, but also mentally going through the process, the various steps. I would inwardly see, hear, and feel myself taking the actions I needed to take, and would then rest in the feeling of my desire as though it were fully accomplished.

I remember sitting on an airplane in late summer of 2005. I was on my way back home to Louisville after a series of performances out west.

I had a rehearsal scheduled one week later and had not yet composed the five songs that we were to rehearse.

I closed my eyes and went in my imagination to First Unitarian Church, where the rehearsals and performance would take place. I imagined the standing ovation at the end of our performance. I took a moment to savor this feeling of accomplishment, then mentally traveled back to the beginning of the concert, where I "saw" and "heard" the essence of each of the five songs that I would write.

I opened my eyes and began writing. By the time the plane landed two hours later, I had first drafts of all five songs, including lyrics. Act as though it were impossible to fail. See and feel your success in advance.

This simple shift in mindset helped a lot.

I still felt resistance, but it didn't have the hold on me that it once did. I would go back to the feeling of successful completion, then imagine myself taking action, and then I would simply start wherever I had left off.

I took this basic principle even deeper.

I would write a short story, dated in the future, that described in detail how I got to the goal.

Here's an example I wrote earlier today, just before I began working on this essay.

It was incredible. It felt so good to save my post today and know that I once again reached my writing goal. I had the chance to apply what I've learned about getting things done from the moment I started. I took the time to imagine myself succeeding, then thought through the obstacles I would most likely face. The biggest one would be time. I had to teach this morning and perform tonight, and I would only have at the very most a little over an hour to get things done. So I made a firm decision to write between two and three fifteen, with only a short break for a stretch. And it worked! I simply kept going. The words flowed with relative ease, and it really feels great now that I am done. Another successful writing day! Thank you, Creator!

I would write a paragraph or two that told the story of specifically how I accomplished the goal, how I dealt with the inevitable obstacles I would face, and how I would feel as a result.

This allowed me to preview the feeling of accomplishment while also beginning to think through potential obstacles and strategize how I might best overcome them.

To summarize my "finish fast formula" principle #1: Begin with the attitude that you will succeed, that you will persist, that you will meet obstacles with creativity and determination, and that you will finish. Envision both your success and the steps you will take on the way.

The second thing I learned?

Make a public commitment to serve.

I really got the power of this principle the week after the terrorist attacks of 9/11 2001.

I had the intuition to organize and promote a concert for peace. I wanted to bring representatives from the various faith traditions together for a tangible demonstration and celebration of our capacity to work together in service of a better world for all.

This idea landed in my brain on September 14, 2001, while attending a memorial service for those who had perished just a few days before.

Less than an hour later, I contacted the School of Music at the University of Louisville to see if they would donate a concert space for a performance to be scheduled in the next few weeks. The only available date on their calendar was October 1, less than three weeks later.

The moment I committed to the space, I had to follow through. The next 17 days were a blur of activity, with me reaching out to different people, organizing rehearsals, and publicizing the concert. Four hundred people showed up to affirm their commitment to a peaceful world.

There are two interrelated aspects to this principle: public commitment and service.

One of my primary values is being of service to others.

I live by George Bernard Shaw's maxim—"I feel that my life belongs to the whole community and I want to serve it as much as I can for as long as I can. I want to be thoroughly used up when I die, for the harder I work, the more I live."

So for the most part, creating for myself or just for a paycheck isn't sufficient to activate my deepest, most powerful source of motivation.

I did learn to create on demand years ago, when I wrote direct response advertising for a living. Deadlines were always my best and dearest friends. I would get the assignment on Wednesday afternoon and the client needed the completed copy by Friday morning. I knew they were counting on me, and I knew that I could not send an invoice unless I came up with the goods. At that time, getting the paycheck was enough to keep me going. Money alone no longer sufficiently lights my inner fire. I now need more to catapult myself beyond my resistance.

On the other hand, creating something for the purpose of serving others gets me fired up.

So when I have an idea for a project, or something I need to finish, I think about who and how it will serve, then make some kind of public commitment. The commitment might be to just one person. And it might be for only a bite-sized piece of a larger project. Last fall, I met a client of master coach Steve Chandler who told me that she got her entire book written by sending Steve one page per day, five days per week, for nearly a year.

So whenever I want to create something, I make a public commitment to serve.

I wrote the choral pieces because I put a concert date on my calendar and I knew people would show up and I needed to have something to show them.

I created the oral history book because I hired someone to sit down with my mother and do the interviews, transcribe, and I am committed to giving her the book as a gift on her 85th birthday later this year.

I wrote the musical because a lot of people were depending on me to come through, and I was committed to the playwright, the actors, the director, and the 26,000 children who were planning to come see it live.

I am writing two thousand words a day because I have committed to post at least one thousand words to my blog every day for the rest of this year. I know that my words touch people and transform their lives, and I have been told by more than one person that they wake every morning looking for my next post.

I have begun to truly master helping people break through the beliefs and blocks that get in the way of living the life of their dreams because I have committed to filling my calendar with classes to take and people to serve.

Whatever I want to create, I schedule a public commitment or performance in service to someone. This literally forces me to completion.

This may not work for everyone. At first, this approach definitely generates a lot of internal pressure. On the other hand, over time, after you've completed a few dozen or a few hundred projects, you begin to have deep inner knowledge that you can and will deliver.

You can adjust the pressure somewhat by not overcommitting or creating deadlines that are so tight that they are impossible.

So how can you develop the habit of finishing?

Make a public commitment, then get started. See and feel your success in advance.

Stay in motion, with an attitude that you will succeed.

Even when you meet with inevitable obstacles, learn, adapt, and keep going.

That's what my GSA student learned to do. A mere three weeks later, the young woman had completed four short stories, eight poems, and had begun her first novel.

Now it's your turn.

Stop reading and get to work.

You've got things to finish.

Chapter 22

The Virtues of Mediocrity

*I hate first drafts, and it never gets easier. People always
wonder what kind of superhero power they'd like to have.
I wanted the ability for someone to just open up my brain and
take out the entire first draft and lay it down in front of me
so I can just focus on the second, third, and fourth drafts.*

—JUDY BLUME

IT IS EXACTLY 7:58 ON SUNDAY MORNING.

I am sitting in the car in my driveway, behind the wheel.

I open the door. It is 85 degrees outside. I just came back from taking my mother to help with a flea market for her church.

And I don't want to write.

I need more sleep.

It's hot.

I'm grumpy.

I only have two hours before I have to get back in the car and go pick her up.

I would rather do anything but write a post right now.

And then the oh-so-familiar broken record starring Mr. Time-for-Another-Excuse starts to play.

Just about every time I sit down to write—poetry, music, or prose—some of these same thoughts will show up. Today it's especially bad because of the time of morning—I am definitely not an early riser when I go to bed at two a.m.—and because of my overall grumpitude.

Why did I commit to doing this—writing 1000 words a day?

What a stupid idea. I don't know where to start. I just can't do this. I'm tired. This is not a good morning for writing. It's too hot.

Why bother? Why am I doing this in the first place? I have nothing to say. I'll wait until tomorrow. Maybe this was a bad idea. It's a beautiful day, I think I'll go take a walk in the park. I have so many books to read. Maybe I'll call up Fred, or Sarah, or Bill, or whomever.

I have got to get out of here—out of this place, this mental space, this feeling, this agony.

And on and on and on.

This broken record of self-judgement. My good friend Mr. Looney Tunes, who means well, but who is just a little off the beam.

For the longest time, these thoughts would stop me cold.

And you know what? After 40 years of active engagement in the creative process, over a million words written, thousands of presentations given, and hundreds of musical works composed, those voices have never gone totally away. And I don't care anymore.

Because I have found the cure.

Here it is.

My cure to stopping the self-sabotaging voices that are always at the ready to get me to quit?

Fully embrace my mediocrity.

That's right. When I give myself permission to write a total piece of crap, guess what happens?

The words begin to flow. Or the notes begin to flow. Or nothing flows and I just write whatever comes into my mind.

But at least I'm in motion.

That's what I did this morning. And boy, the first half-page of drivel I wrote was god-awful. But I didn't stop.

I just showed up.

And 75 minutes later, I was done with a post that evoked tears of joy and gratitude in the person I wrote about when he read it. "No one has ever captured my essence in words like you did. I am in tears," he emailed me a few hours later.

And that's really the bottom line. If you want to create anything of value, start by just showing up.

That's the secret.

I put words or notes on paper (or a keyboard). And once I start, I keep going until my agreed-upon time is up. That might mean writing in a 10-minute burst; or a 30- or 45-minute segment. Sometimes I will keep going for a couple of hours if I'm on a roll. When I'm composing, I give myself half-day (four-hour) blocks of time to work.

This morning I wrote from eight to nine fifteen—while sitting in the car in my driveway with the door open.

The number-one rule is simple: don't stop. And don't evaluate—yet. Just "darken the page" as Steve Chandler says.

And above all, let go of those insane ideas about how good it has to be. That's the job of the editor, the craftsperson, the refiner inside you, who can't do their job without raw material to work with.

One of my favorite books for jump-starting the creative process, *The Frustrated Songwriters Handbook*, recommends a friendly competition where you and a partner each write 20 songs in a day, sharing your work at day's end.

I know, sounds crazy. And it really works. When you have to crank out a new song (or a new blog post, or a new painting, or a new monologue) every 30 to 40 minutes, your internal judge doesn't have time to do its thing.

Central to the game is to forget about quality completely.

That's right.

The idea is to write 20 bad songs.

And the funny thing is, when you set out to write something bad 20 times in a row, the likelihood of you coming up with something good increases exponentially.

But you've got to be willing to accept total mediocrity first. (Attention: I am not advocating mediocrity in the end product. Heaven knows, there's enough bad writing and music and poetry and art or whatever out there, created by well-meaning but undisciplined or unaware folks who don't adequately refine their work.)

* * *

The place for high standards comes in two phases—in taking the time to do the initial pre-work—for writing prose, making sure my outline, my information, my examples are sound and coherent and logical; for music, getting clear on the text, the genre, the basic structure.

The other place for high standards is in the editing and refining phase, where everything is once again up for grabs.

But not while I'm creating.

Forget the standards, the judgements, the comparisons with anyone and anything past or present, including myself and my own work. Not while the ideas are flowing. Not while I'm improvising those first themes which might go here, there, or anywhere.

That phase is bound to be mediocre, so I stop judging it. I'm happily, delightfully, authentically awful.

Then, as I keep on going, and stay in the game, eventually I can mold and shape whatever raw material has emerged into something coherent, elegant, and even beautiful.

When I go back over first and second drafts for some of my posts or essays, or my early sketches for original songs, I notice how rarely the first impulse ends up as part of the final work.

My most recent major composing commission was a suite of pieces based on a dozen poems by Wendell Berry. For at least three of these, my first melodies and concepts were so awful I almost screamed when I listened back to them. When I review those sketches now, it's almost laughable how bad they were.

But I knew the first few tries would most likely stink, so I just accepted that. I didn't allow the horrific sounds that I was making to get through to my sense of self-worth, because I know you don't get to the goodies without the grit.

Eventually, with diligence, willingness to throw out what wasn't working, and trust in the process, I found the mood, themes, structure, and setting that worked for each poem.

The more I produce, the more certain I become that the muse grants her greatest gifts to those who are willing to simply do the work. To set the stage for grace. To create context and containers for creativity to flourish.

And to stop judging and let go of any and all desire for quality—during this initial creative phase.

Everything stinks before it succeeds. So give yourself permission to be wildly, fiercely mediocre.

Just don't stop there.

Chapter 23

Just Punch the Clock

Do it badly; do it slowly; do it fearfully;
do it any way you have to, but do it.
—STEVE CHANDLER

THIS MORNING A FRIEND CONFIDED IN ME ABOUT WHAT A rough time she was having getting motivated to write these days.

"I just don't feel like it," she exclaimed. "I want to write, but I just don't feel inspired."

I took a breath and paused for a moment.

"So, what does inspiration have to do with writing?"

Silence.

"Well, don't great writers write from a state of inspiration?"

"I don't know. Do they?"

My friend actually knew better. A decade before, she had a successful career as a freelance copywriter, with impossible deadlines thrown at her week after week. In the past few years, she had succeeded both in running a consulting business and raising a beautiful daughter.

"You know all that copy you wrote for all those years? Did you wait for inspiration?"

She laughed. "No. My inspiration was the fat check I would get in the mail once the job was done."

"Exactly. Did you do good work?"

"I actually did great work. Sold a lot of stuff. Earned a few awards. Made good money, too."

"So you already know the secret. You just forgot."

"Well, remind me. What's the secret?"

"The inspiration comes sooner or later when you just show up day after day and do the work."

"Yeah. You're right. Thanks for the reminder."

Show up. Do the work.

Punch the clock.

Truck drivers don't waste time and energy deciding if they feel like driving today. The guy or gal who works on the assembly line at the Ford factory doesn't spend two nanoseconds debating whether they feel like going to work.

Or, even if they do, that debate has only one conclusion.

Get up, hit the road, punch the clock, get paid.

Why should creating music or art or prose or poetry or theater be so different?

How did we get seduced into this idea that emotions, feelings, or mystical, magical states of inspiration need to determine when we work, how we work, and or if we work on whatever we have chosen as our predominant creative expression?

Why in the world do we act as though we are helpless in the face of a lousy mood or self-critical voice in our heads?

Writer and entrepreneur Steve Chandler has written more than 30 books in the past 15 years. I attended a creativity and writing seminar with Steve and was astonished to hear him say that, on average, he writes for only one hour a day.

His only goal each day? "To darken the page."

In other words, he's punching the clock. Showing up and doing the work.

So many would-be artists, musicians, writers, poets, actors, and what-have-you never really get this.

Creativity, like any other skill, is built one song, one poem, one painting, one work at a time.

The more you do, the better you get.

Don't wait for the right mood. You'll be waiting a long time.

Instead, just punch the clock.

Put in the time.

Show up.

Darken the page.

PART VI

In Tune with Adversity

GROWING THROUGH CHALLENGE

Chapter 24

Harmony from Heartbreak

The walls we build around us to
keep sadness out also keep out the joy.
—JIM ROHN

FRIDAY MORNING, 2:08 A.M. MY FOURTH SLEEPLESS NIGHT IN A week.

I dragged myself out of bed and downstairs where my Yamaha upright piano waited in the living room.

I had been so in love (or so I thought). Until I learned the truth.

The higher you fly, the harder you fall.

My heart shattered into a million pieces.

I sat down on the piano bench, lost in sadness, and began to play (and sing) the three most depressing odes to lost love that I knew: "Lush Life," "Everything Happens to Me," and "You Don't Know What Love Is."

Over and over and over again for the next two hours.

The next morning, again awake at two, I did it again.

And the next morning.

And the next.

Always between two and four a.m.

For three weeks in a row.

Each time, I would sing along, my voice cracking, phrases melting into uncontrollable sobs.

Then you came along with your siren song
To tempt me to madness!
I thought for a while that your poignant smile was tinged with
    the sadness
Of a great love for me.

I guess (Ah yes!) I was wrong
Again, I was wrong.

Life (sniff) *is lonely again* (sniff),
and only last year everything seemed so sure (wail, sob).
Now life is awful again, (I stop, head in hands, to weep for a
    while, then continue)
A trough full of hearts could only be a bore.[1]

Every morning I sang and played my weeping willow wretchedness.

I've telegraphed and phoned;
I sent airmail special, too;
Your answer was goodbye,
And there was even postage due.
I fell in love just once;

---

1 "Lush Life." Lyrics by Billy Strayhorn. Copyright Billy Strayhorn Songs (ASCAP). Used by permission.

And then it had to be with you,
Everything happens to me.[2]

Every morning I woke to the same sobbing sorrow.

These three songs became my mantras of misery for three weeks, in the wee small hours of each morning.

And then it was over. I had sung and played my grief until it was all drained out. I was done. I felt lighter, clearer, whole again. I could now move on with my life. Perhaps I would one day love again.

But something else had changed.

I used to rush through ballads, filling every crack and crevice with quasi-virtuoso scales, arpeggios, and flourishes. I couldn't wait to get done with the slow song and back to something faster and flashier.

But ballads held a new meaning for me now. And my playing showed it.

A new maturity, a richer quality of heart, a deeper lyricism. Each phrase had more depth and meaning. I no longer needed to attempt to spin endless virtuoso variations.

A beautiful melody, sensitively stated, was more than enough.

No more extra notes.

Heartbreak transformed into harmony.

Until that moment, I hadn't fully appreciated the musical necessity of a rich emotional life. My playing, always somewhat technically proficient, was often emotionally lacking. But once my heart cracked open, I found myself able to express much

---

2 "Everything Happens to Me." Lyrics by Tom Adair. Copyright Warner/ Chappell Music, Inc. Used by permission.

more of the bittersweet quality hidden in these immortal love songs.

I finally was beginning to understand Charlie Parker's wisdom, when he said: "Music is your own experience, your thoughts, your wisdom. If you don't live it, it won't come out of your horn."

My playing would now touch others more powerfully because they would feel my authentic emotional truth communicated through the notes.

It seems that every life experience, even the most difficult, can open the door to deeper, more authentic artistic expression.

We may play with the hands, but ultimately, we play from the heart.

Chapter 25

Adversity to Advantage

Adversity is like a strong wind. It tears away
from us all but the things that cannot be torn,
so that we see ourselves as we really are.

—ARTHUR GOLDEN

IT HAPPENED SO FAST.

One minute I was walking out the front door of the Best Western Hotel near downtown Greensboro, North Carolina. The next instant, I was flat on the ground, my neck throbbing in pain.

I was visiting Greensboro to spend three days teaching at UNCG, where my friend, colleague, and kick-ass drummer, Thomas Taylor, was on faculty.

I was really looking forward to this short residency. UNCG has a great jazz program and it always thrilled me to share ideas and energy with young musicians.

It was a dreary, rainy day, and I guess my foot slipped as I walked along the slick marble entryway on my way to Thomas's waiting car.

As I fell, at least I had the presence of mind to turn my head to the left, so I didn't smash my face. My glasses went flying, and I felt a numb yet intense pain across the back of my neck, extending down my left arm and side.

I was obviously not going to teach today.

Thomas had watched my awkward fall from the driver's seat and quickly jumped out of the car to help me to my feet. Back in the hotel room, Thomas and I researched local chiropractors, and we found someone who could see me later that morning.

An X-ray indicated no permanent damage, and between the chiropractic adjustments and icing my neck and shoulder, I felt perhaps 20 percent better.

Definitely no teaching that day, though.

We went back to the hotel and I slumped into the lounge chair by the bed, still stunned by what had happened. Of course, it could have been worse. I could have broken my nose, or sprained my wrist, or . . . who knows?

I said goodbye to Thomas, and settled in for a day of recovery.

As I sat there, dreary and frustrated, sore and confused, I wondered, what now? How am I going to make it through these next three days?

I remembered a quote by Napoleon Hill, author of many books on success, including the best-selling *Think and Grow Rich*. Hill wrote, "Every adversity contains within it the seed of an equivalent or greater benefit."

I began to reflect.

So, how does this apply to me right now in this moment here in this hotel room, my neck aching, my head throbbing?

Why did this happen? What's the lesson? What's the gift? What's the greater benefit that could come from this?

Almost immediately came the insight: stop focusing simply on music, on techniques and practices and disciplines and preparation and performance.

Use this accident and this opportunity to go deeper. Deeper than you've ever gone before in your interactions with these young musicians.

Talk to the students about what really matters.

Teach life. Help them develop a personal philosophy that helps transform adversity into advantage, just like the opportunity you are facing right now with this injury. Get real. Be more authentic in connecting a life in music with the music of life.

Wow.

What an opportunity.

The students already respected and listened to me because of my musical skills. I could leverage that positive attention and share essential principles for living. I felt a quiet excitement rising within me even in the midst of the physical pain.

From now on, I would consciously, intentionally, and systematically integrate music with life—and life with music.

From here on out, musical principles would be used to teach about what really matters.

I returned to the chiropractor every morning for the duration of my Greensboro trip, then went to the school to teach.

The workshops and lessons went well, in spite of my still considerable stiffness and soreness.

I continued to follow my inner guidance, sharing more deeply and personally than ever before. I talked about the essential questions one must eventually address in order to craft a life of meaning from whatever circumstances one might face.

How does one proceed in the face of life's challenges? What do you need to do to get clear about what really matters to you? How does one begin to create a life of meaning? How do you develop a philosophy that sees obstacles as opportunities?

Even though I didn't expect and certainly didn't ask for such an inauspicious beginning to my Greensboro visit, the accident had a silver lining.

I see now, 16 years later, that this was a turning point for me.

For the first time, I taught principles for living a meaningful life right alongside principles for developing musical proficiency.

My fall thrust me by necessity into a new perspective and a deeper alignment with what really matters.

Thank you, Napoleon Hill, for this pearl of wisdom that continues to transform my life.

"Every adversity contains within it the seed of an equivalent or greater benefit."

Chapter 26

The Gift Has Landed

No teacher, preacher, parent, friend
Or wise man can decide
What's right for you—just listen to
The voice that speaks inside.

—SHEL SILVERSTEIN

"YOU'RE A GIFT LOOKING FOR A PLACE TO LAND."

Joyce Wycoff was my neighbor in the Tierrasanta community of San Diego. She was a brilliant author and an expert on innovation. I had requested her feedback on a decision I was facing. My desire to do many things at once was getting the best of me.

Ever since I was a child, I had been both blessed and cursed by two seemingly contradictory compulsions.

On the one hand, I have always displayed a remarkable ability to "learn by obsession."

Get me a goldfish and I would bug my mom until she took me to the library and helped me check out stacks of books. I became an obnoxious eight-year-old expert on the marine kingdom. Just call me Harry "Jacques Cousteau" Pickens.

The same was true with collecting comic books, learning American history, listening to radio mysteries, exploring the world of orchestral music. Whatever I was into, I would go deep and fast and as far as I possibly could—for a few months. Total, complete, obsessional focus.

Then I would let it go and go on to the next thing.

The second trait was a kind of compulsive curiosity about everything.

I was passionately interested in astrology, archeology, biology, botany, chemistry, geology, model airplanes, architecture, baseball cards, stamp and coin collecting, science fiction, and world religions, in addition to the subjects already mentioned.

I was also drawn to philosophy and metaphysics. I have no idea how I ever learned about yoga or cosmic consciousness in the tiny conservative Southeast Georgia coastal town I grew up in, but I did.

And of course, this was before easy access to a world of information via smartphone or laptop. Exploring these curiosities required trips to libraries, bookstores, museums, and concerts (plus lots of hours watching public television). I pursued this catholic curiosity with a fervor and passion that was unstoppable.

So on the one hand, I could focus like a laser beam on whatever struck my fancy; on the other hand, I was constantly interested in everything.

This union of opposites within me did not sit well in a culture of specialization, where when you're a child everyone asks you the same question.

"So, what do you want to be when you grow up?"

As though there was only one thing I could be and I had to choose.

Even then, I was like Buckminster Fuller—I was a verb, not a noun. Always growing and changing and morphing and transforming into ever-new forms and ever-new identities, with ever-new interests and desires and passions and curiosities.

Renowned career coach Barbara Sher found that approximately 15 to 20 percent of the thousands whom she helped to create fulfilling professional lives were like me. She called them scanners.

Scanners have multiple, often competing interests. They not only refuse to choose, they are constitutionally unable to choose.

To choose one passion over the other would be like favoring your liver over your heart, or your left foot over your right hand. How can one possibly neglect an essential part of one's psychic anatomy?

But refusing to choose came at a cost.

* * *

"Well, with this résumé I figured you just couldn't keep a job."

I felt my heart sink into my gut with shame when he said those words. Sure, my résumé was non-traditional. I'd created a half-dozen careers in the two decades since I'd finished college. And I'd been successful in every one.

But there was that old familiar sense of embarrassment. What was wrong with me? Why couldn't I just fit in? Why did I have to be so different? Where did I go wrong?

We were planning an executive retreat and he was a junior partner in one of the companies I'd be working with. I brought along a vita as requested as part of our getting-to-know-you exercise, so that we could learn more about the strengths we were each bringing to the team. (Obviously, this was pre-Google and LinkedIn.) The other participants included ex-military officers, CEOs, and a couple of seasoned consultants.

I was brought in to talk about the unique mindsets required for effective collaboration in an improvisational art form like jazz, and the corresponding insights that might help teams meet the challenges of rapid and unpredictable change.

To this day, I don't know what was going on inside him that would generate such a comment. Maybe he didn't like me. Maybe he was testing to see how I would respond. Maybe he was envious of what looked to him like my freedom to think out of the box that he had lived in for decades.

What I do know was it triggered that old wound that had been festering inside me for a long time.

I didn't yet know about Barbara's scanners. All I knew was that I simply didn't fit in—anywhere.

I didn't fit in with most people of any single ethnicity, although the blood of African slaves and Native peoples and European conquerors all ran through my veins.

I didn't fit in with many of musicians I knew and worked with at the time, whose interests outside of music tended not to be very far-ranging.

I didn't fit in with many people who worked a 9-to-5 job, because I didn't relate to their notion of the creative demands and financial insecurities of my freelance lifestyle.

I didn't fit in with many entrepreneurs, who tended to lean further to the right politically and to see the world a bit too much through profit-and-loss lenses for my taste.

I hated the phrase "jack-of-all-trades, master of none," because that is how I felt people tended to interpret my wide-ranging interests and multiple, sometimes simultaneous careers.

The truth is I had invested thousands of hours over the decades to work towards mastery in several fields—music, teaching, facilitation, marketing, copywriting. But somehow, I still felt lost—at least in the eyes of mainstream society.

A gift looking for a place to land.

Those words never left me. I wondered if I would ever land. Would I ever find peace with these different parts of myself? I knew that I felt most alive when I was learning and growing, and when my different interests could feed off one another. I loved them all.

Finally, after years of searching, exploring, looking for, and finding others like me—who could not settle on one career, one profession, one job, one way of working in the world—I found what I had been searching for.

Joyce had been right all along.

I was searching for a place to land.

But it was not an external place. Rather, it was a place inside of me. A sanctuary of identity where I could rest at last. A place within my soul that could declare unashamedly and unabashedly: Here I stand. This is who I am. Here is what matters to me. Here is how I express myself in service in the world. My means of authentic self-expression does not look like anyone else's—because it is mine alone. You have never before seen anything like it—because it reflects my unique identity, my particular refraction of the Light that illumines all Creation. And it's all me.

Finally, I've landed.

I know now that my compulsive curiosity and laser focus rest at the very center of my greatest gifts to the world.

I know now that I do not have to answer to any voice outside of me that would attempt to question or belittle my diverse passions, my capacity to see from multiple and divergent perspectives, and my interest in a bigger and broader perspective than any single discipline can offer.

I know now that I was born to be a master of many trades, and a first-rate me, not a second-rate anyone else.

Thank you, Joyce.

The gift has found its home.

PART VII

In Tune with Love

BECOMING AN INSTRUMENT

Chapter 27

Remember the Love

Music is love made audible.

—WILLIAM A. SEYMOUR

I RECOGNIZED HER JUST AS SHE PASSED THE OLD HEINE Brothers Coffee Shop. I was walking west on the south side of Bardstown Road, just east of Eastern Parkway.

She was across the street walking in the opposite direction. Head down, she seemed sad, lost in her own world. I waved and yelled out.

"Sandy!"

She looked up, saw me, and smiled.

I crossed the street to say hello.

"Hi there," she said. "How are you doing?"

"I'm okay. How are you?"

"I'm good."

"I know we talked about getting together for a lesson or just to talk about music, and I want you to know I live right down the block. If you're free later this afternoon, please drop by."

"That would be great! I'd like that."

"Okay."

I wrote down my address and phone number on a scrap piece of paper and handed it to her.

"Here. I'm around. Just call or stop by."

"Okay, I will."

* * *

About two hours later, she knocked on my door.

"Hello, Sandy! How are you? Please come in. Have a seat. So how is music school?"

"Well, it's okay."

"Only okay? Tell me more."

"It's actually pretty hard right now. All the theory and classes. I don't have enough time to practice. And I really don't know if I want to do music anymore."

Sandy was a sophomore. A gifted pianist, she received a full scholarship to attend the University of Louisville School of Music from her home country of Ecuador. I first met her nearly a year before when she introduced herself right after one of my jazz trio concerts at the university.

When I learned that she was a pianist, I asked if she would play for me. She sat at the piano and shared the third movement of Ravel's "Sonatine" with me, playing with technical assurance and deep beauty. I had seen her around campus several times since then, but we never exchanged more than a hello—until today.

"Wow. I'm sorry to hear that. What do you think is happening?"

"I don't know. It just doesn't feel the same."

"I'm sorry. Well, since you're here, and I have this piano, would you like to play for me?"

"Sure. Would you play something, too?"

"Of course. Would you like for me to go first?"

"Yes."

I felt her shyness, and thought my playing first might help her relax. Perhaps after she played, we could also get down to the important conversation about her love for music.

"You've already heard me play jazz, so I would like to play some Chopin for you. Would that be all right?"

"Yes."

"Great. This is Opus 64, number 1 in Ab major."

"That was really beautiful."

I looked up and saw tears welling in her eyes.

"Are you okay?"

"Yes, it is just so beautiful how you play."

"Well, for you to even recognize that beauty, you must have it in yourself. Would you play for me now?"

"Yes."

She played Schubert for me—a sonata movement, perhaps.

"That is so beautiful. You play with such feeling and tenderness."

"Really?"

"Yes, really. So what has happened to your love for music?"

She sighed. "I don't really know. It's just so much work to get it right."

I stopped her. "Who do you play for?"

"What do you mean? Who?"

"Who do you play for?"

"The people who come to hear me, my teachers, the other students."

"And you think about them?"

"Yes."

"Well, that is exactly your problem."

"I'm confused. What do you mean?"

"Of course. And that confusion is why you are suffering. Let me explain. You're in school where all of the focus is on the technical aspects of playing, and on getting it right and perfect, and on getting the grades, and on all of these other things that have very little to do with the heart and soul of music. No wonder you are forgetting what really matters! As long as you are trying to please anyone else—your teachers, your audience, your peers—you are neglecting the most important person—yourself. So, I have a question. What if you did not care what anyone outside of you thought about your playing? How would you play? How would you feel?"

"Relieved."

"Exactly. So play the beginning of this piece once again. But don't play it to impress me. Just play for you. To feed your soul with beauty.

"How did that feel?"

"Much better."

"Sandy, this happens to most music students. They get so fixated on technical perfection and on doing things right and on getting the grades, that they forget why they make music in the first place. You are a musician because you fell in love. You fell in love with sound! You fell in love with this marvelous instrument! You fell in love with the beauty and power and magic revealed by Ravel and Schubert and Mozart and all the others. So your number-one job is to remember that love, to feel that love, to express that love in every note you play.

"Take a moment right now to think about your love for this piece, for the piano, for the privilege of music. Now play. That was much better. Did you feel the difference?"

"Oh yes. Totally different. I feel connected again. Like I felt when I was much younger. No worries or concerns."

"Exactly. Now staying connected to this feeling does not mean you ignore your teacher's instruction, or you stop practicing, or you play with sloppy technique. It means that all of your focus is directed on coming back to this place—the place of simply remembering why you play in the first place—and reconnecting with that love."

Sandy left my apartment that day walking taller, feeling better about herself and her musical future.

So simple once we see it, yet so easy to forget.

Remember the love.

Let that be the soil out of which the flowers of your musical expression may grow and blossom.

Chapter 28

Instruments

*Music is only a mystery to people who want it
explained. Music and love are the same.*
—SIMON VAN BOOY

EVEN AS THE MUSIC PLAYED, YOU COULD FEEL THE SILENCE.

It was an inner silence of full attention, of deep presence, of singular focus.

A quality of listening that swept away mind's chatter, opening the heart to shared stillness.

I didn't feel as though I was "playing" the piano. Nor was Chris playing the bass, or Meg playing drums.

No.

Instead, we were now the instruments as music played itself through us.

Instruments of healing. Instruments of harmony.

Instruments of love.

The song, the musical vessel through which this love flowed, was Sting's "Fragile," which speaks poignantly to the preciousness and fragility of life.

We were there for the first evening performance of the 2015 Kentucky Governor's School for the Arts.

It was only 10 days after the massacre in Charleston, South Carolina, and the song was dedicated to those nine who lost their lives and to their families and loved ones they left behind.

I requested that, as the song played, the nearly 300 students, faculty, and staff present focus their intention and attention on transmitting an energy of healing and compassion to those in Charleston who were suffering.

And we could feel it in the air.

Wave after wave of love, carried on the wings of music, intended to touch those so far away, to lift them up and to bring to them a moment of solace, of peace, of comfort in the midst of their grief.

What else is music for?

*   *   *

The worship service was nearly over.

Now an even deeper transmission of grace would begin.

Mother had the touch. Her postlude began after the benediction, and the church sat silently until she finished. Those final four or five minutes made sitting through the whole service worthwhile.

Honestly, as a child and teenager, I always felt more of the living presence of God in the music than in all the words spoken (and there were a lot of them).

The hymns became my theology—rather, they were the way theology came alive inside of me. And the hymns Mother played during those postludes—how they spoke to my heart!

"How Great Thou Art."

"Soon I Will Be Done."

"Precious Lord."

"Peace Be Still."

"In the Garden."

The living waters of the Gospel—flowing through her fingertips.

I loved the way she would pause just a bit at the end of each phrase.

She was breathing. Breathing along with the phrases, singing on the inside.

Years later, I asked her: "Mother, how did you do that? How did you make people cry Sunday after Sunday with the purity and beauty of those simple hymns?"

Her response was stark.

"Harry, I play the words. I always think the words of the hymn and sing along in my mind and heart when I play. I never focus on the notes—it's all about the words."

That was Mother's secret.

Play the words, not the notes.

My first experience of the musician as instrument.

Instrument of love.

*   *   *

"I am a hole in a flute that the Christ's breath
moves through. Listen to this music."
—HAFEZ

What greater purpose for the musician than to allow himself or herself to become an instrument for the transmission of love?

And it can be so simple.

First, set the intention that every note you play or sing will carry the energy of love, of harmony, of beauty, of compassion wherever you direct it.

Once you begin, forget about the notes. Forget about yourself. Forget about anyone who might happen to be listening.

Imagine yourself as the instrument, as the vehicle for transmitting this sweet fragrance of loving-kindness through the vehicle of sound.

The more you practice playing or singing with this intention, the more your music making will be filled with this strange and intangible grace, which will be felt by all those who hear you.

Learn the notes. Become technically proficient. Commit to mastery. Then let it all go.

Go beyond the notes to that pure and sacred and spacious silence within from which music is born. Then your entire body and being will have become the instrument. And the music you bring forth will ride on wings of love.

> *"Lord, make me an instrument . . ."*
> —PRAYER OF ST. FRANCIS

*   *   *

The last note of "Fragile" slowly fades away.
Then, a moment of silence before the explosion of applause.
The song is over.
The love remains.

Chapter 29

Ageless Communion

*Music is the social act of communication among people,
a gesture of friendship, the strongest there is.*

—MALCOLM ARNOLD

I FOUND THE PICTURE JUST THE OTHER DAY.

Me at the piano.

And the Chopin lady.

I was visiting the assisted living home to share a bit of music on that cloudy Saturday afternoon.

There was barely enough space in the tiny sitting room for the piano plus the 20 or so who came downstairs that day. Spread around the room on the paisley-upholstered Victorian couches and chairs, they ranged in age from their early 70s to mid-90s; some in robust health, others quite frail. A few were in wheelchairs. All seemed excited to hear me play.

This was my third visit to Mayfair Village. Mary, who volunteered at Mayfair and was a gifted artist and musician who occasionally brought her flute and played for the residents, had first invited me nearly a year before.

I met Mary through her husband Bob, one of the finest

photographers I've known. The first time he showed me prints of his photos of my quartet playing at an outdoor music festival, I was blown away. I would see Bob often when I performed in Lexington, and was saddened by his untimely passing just a few years later.

One day after a concert, Mary mentioned Mayfair Village, and thought that the residents would really enjoy my playing. Would I be willing to drop by sometimes? Of course.

Usually there would be a dozen or so folks gathered in the little sitting room. I would play, tell a story or two, and listen to a story or two. I would perform songs from the Tin Pan Alley repertoire, songs that they grew up with and would usually recognize. Gershwin. Cole Porter. Irving Berlin. Duke Ellington.

I loved seeing these elders come alive, heads bobbing, lips moving as they mouthed the words. Of course, not everyone remembered so well, but their smiles of delight were more than enough to keep me going.

After about 45 minutes that day, I had completed my set but was in no hurry to leave. After the room cleared out, a handful—four or five folks—stayed around.

My attention was drawn to one lady in particular.

She sat over in the corner in her wheelchair, her thick gray hair neatly combed in a bun. Her penetrating yet sad blue eyes were fixed on the piano keyboard.

She noticed my glance and looked up.

"So what kind of music do you like?"

She spoke quietly, almost in a whisper. "I like classical music."

"Wonderful. Who's your favorite composer?"

Without hesitation, she responded, "Chopin."

"Chopin? Really? May I play some Chopin for you?"

She nodded. "Okay."

"Great. Would you mind coming closer to the piano?"

An attendant wheeled her over so that she was just about a foot away.

"That's much better. You'll enjoy it more this way, because this is just for you."

I closed my eyes and began to play Chopin's waltz in Ab major, Opus 69, number 1.

Within seconds, I felt it. Something unusual was happening.

What's going on?

Oh. I know. It's her.

I could actually feel this lady listening to the music.

Truly, deeply listening.

Listening with her heart and soul.

Listening with total presence, attention, intensity.

It felt like she was drinking the music in with every cell of her being. I'd never experienced anything quite like this—this profound exchange between my playing and another's listening.

As the music continued, I found myself entering into one of the deepest internal states of quiet, focused presence I'd ever felt. All boundaries dissolved between me, the piano, the music, and this person whom I had met only moments before.

The intimacy was almost overwhelming. We were together, as one, drinking in the sweet nectar of Chopin. All else disappeared for those precious moments.

The music ceased. I rested my hands on my lap. Eyes still closed, just taking in the rich silence evoked by the music.

After a moment, I returned from wherever I was. I opened my eyes and looked at her. Our eyes met. I took her hand. We sat together in silence for another moment.

Our moment of mystical musical union continued. There was

no old lady in a wheelchair, no piano, no me. Just the presence of love.

"Thank you," she whispered. I nodded.

"It was nice to meet you." I reached over to give her a hug, still a bit stunned by what had just occurred.

I had never before felt someone listening with such intensity.

This dear lady seemed hungry, desperately hungry, for the nourishment that only music could provide.

And her hunger evoked something in me that would forever shift my understanding of the relationship between performer and listener.

I learned later that she had been living at Mayfair Village for many years, had been very ill, and was a bit of a recluse, rarely leaving her room. The fact that she came downstairs at all was unusual. She was once a gifted pianist and a teacher of piano. Perhaps that explained the intensity I felt when she was taking in the music.

Until that moment in that tiny room at Mayfair Village, I didn't realize how much the listener's presence and attention could impact my experience as a performer.

Now I understand.

There is always an exchange when we share the gift of music.

Those who listen deeply feed our souls, just as the music we share feeds theirs.

Chapter 30

Only This

Music is Love in search of a word.
—SIDNEY LANIER

THIS IS A TRANSCRIPT OF A SKYPE CHAT WITH A FORMER student. She had been struggling with her relationship to music, particularly in terms of her feelings of self-judgement and perfectionism.

There is something very specific that I wanted to ask you, because perhaps you can understand, or give me a better idea of what's going on and how I can start to manage it.

Okay.

I have noticed that I feel really angry in relation to music.

Yes? Tell me more.

Sure. Especially when things don't come out the way I want. It's hard not to feel it. I am not very gracious about what I do that I am not satisfied with.

I don't like this. I want to enjoy things. I want to be happy, even if things don't come out the way I want them to come out.

It is important to me because music shouldn't do this to anyone. There's a lot of judgment that I can't seem to get rid of.

When have you felt this most strongly? Did you feel this before you went back to school for your master's?

Yes. I think I've felt this way my whole musical life, at least after I started feeling the pressure to be better.

Going to graduate school actually helped me because I got to play with incredible musicians, some of who happen to have beautiful souls, and who were always happy and gracious about things. Some of them, anyway :)

Did you feel this way when you visited Louisville last year and we were making music together?

No. Never felt that around you. What I'm saying is that I want to find a way to never feel like this—this anger, this self-judgement— ever again. I just want to be happy playing music.

Lately I barely listen to music. And my desire to play is just beginning to come back slowly now after four months of being sick and not wanting to play at all.

Okay. I got it. Let me share something that helped me. Maybe it will help you.

At one point in my musical life, I had to get honest with myself. I realized that I would never be a virtuoso—at least not on the level of some of my idols—and that I would never play the piano quite as well as I had hoped.

Yes?

For many years, I rarely really enjoyed playing. And when it did feel good, I quickly returned to a dark place of self-doubt, frustration, and seemingly permanent dissatisfaction and anxiety.

In fact, two or three times in the past couple of decades,

I've simply taken time—sometimes months, sometimes years—away from music because I needed to release my attachment to this feeling that I would never be the musician I once dreamed of being.

But then something began to shift.

After many years of struggle—musically, personally, and spiritually—I had a realization that changed everything.

Part of it came as a result of being chronically ill for almost a decade—and actually losing quite a bit of concentration and fine-motor coordination, so that for years, I literally could not focus well enough to play at a high level.

I actually had to face the fact that I might never play the piano really well again.

Part of this realization came as a result of being forced to confront myself, my ego, and my need for the approval of others, particularly other musicians who I felt so competitive with and often inferior to.

As a result, I finally came to understand that only one thing really mattered for me musically: the way people felt when I played for them.

Yes.

It didn't matter if I was playing a folk ballad, or a jazz standard, or a hymn, or a classical sonata, or a pop song.

All of my virtuosity and perfectionism—that I was so obsessed with—did not really matter.

Because all of that technical stuff was just a means to an end, and something I had given way too much importance to in my confused state.

And even though I knew I would never be a virtuoso on the level I had hoped, maybe my real gift was a simpler one.

And what was that?

Maybe my gift was just to love people—one note at a time.

Oh. I see.

I've been lucky to have had a lot of different experiences playing music.

I have played in famous jazz clubs all around the world.

I have played for people who were very sick—some dying— often within a few days or weeks of their death.

I have played for little children who were bubbling with joy.

I have played for people who were sad and in the depths of grief.

I have played for wealthy people in huge mansions on nine-foot conservatory concert grand pianos.

I have played in tiny little living rooms on rickety spinet pianos that had not been tuned for 20 years.

I have played in homeless shelters for people whose lives were filled with desperation and despair.

I have played in big-shot concert halls and festivals before tens of thousands of people.

I have played in nursing homes for people in wheelchairs who needed oxygen tanks to breathe.

And through all these experiences—you know what I realized?

What's that?

It's all the same.

All.

The.

Same.

Because when I focus simply on loving people through the music, it doesn't matter what I *can't* play. It doesn't matter if I'm playing jazz, or folk, or classical, or country, or chant. It doesn't matter if I'm playing for one person or 20,000 people.

Just like when you're giving somebody a hug, it doesn't matter how tall or short you are.

What matters in that moment is your presence, your love, your heart. That's how I see music now. If I had to choose, I would rather be a virtuoso at loving and kindness than a virtuoso at the piano. Does that help a little bit?

What a beautiful way to see things. Yes, it helps.

It's like here with my mother. She had to go to the emergency room three nights ago, because she had been feeling weak and exhausted for a couple of days.

Oh! How is she?

She's okay now. But from the time I saw her that morning, my whole day shifted.

I had plans for the day. I had places to go, people to connect with, things to do. I was excited about the day that stretched before me, because I knew it was going to be a productive day.

Then I went into her room. I knew something was wrong, and my priorities had to shift—right away. I dropped my plans.

Yes.

I chose to focus on her. I chose to do everything I could to help her. And my real job in caring for my mother that day?

What was that?

Just this. To show up and love. Nothing more. Nothing less.

I get it.

So for me, playing the piano, caring for my mother, talking with you, teaching a class, walking the dog, making turkey chili, or writing a blog post—these are ultimately *all the same.*

In every case, my job is simple. Show up and love. That releases the pressure of perfection.

This doesn't negate—in the realm of music—doing the work of practicing, preparing, paying attention to detail, moving in the direction of mastery.

This is not an excuse for neglecting essential elements of musicianship and proficiency or the value of disciplined effort. But it places the emphasis in a different place.

This sounds so simple, and I do understand your basic point. But don't you ever feel afraid, or confused, or insecure or not good enough?

Of course I do.

Sometimes I am afraid.

Sometimes I feel discouraged and doubtful.

Sometimes I think I'm not as good as whoever.

Occasionally I wonder if I made a mistake trying to play the piano in the first place.

But I go back to my heart and I remember my job.

I'm here to show up and love.

And I make a conscious choice. So that's what I pour into the piano. That's what I pour into this conversation. That's what I pour into these words. That's what I pour into every action, every interaction, every note.

Just love—to the fullest of my ability.

Here's one more thing to remember.

One day, at the end of your life, you will have played perhaps millions of notes of music.

When you look back, from the perspective of your final moments, you won't care so much about how many notes you played or what songs you played or even who you played for.

You *will* care about how much love was in the notes. Period.

Yes. That feels like what I need.

So why not care about that *now*?

It is funny now that I think of it, I rarely want to listen to music, but I put on your music a lot yesterday.

Yes. That makes sense. I'm glad my music helped you. That is the greatest gift for me to know. Because I want it—my music— to be like a big warm blanket of love that just wraps around you and reminds you that you are okay, that you are loved, and that life is good—even in the midst of the crazy.

Well, that is how it feels. And it also reminds me that there is a deeper meaning in all things.

Good. *That* is what music is for.

Just giving *that* gift to people.

Just transmitting *that* tiny ray of love and light—one note at a time.

Nobody really cares about you being a virtuoso or doing it perfectly all the time. (Except a couple of critics, some of your fellow musicians and a few professors!) All the rest of the people—the other 99 percent—simply want to feel the love inside the notes, you see?

I see.

So just play for the people! It took me 50 years to finally figure this out.

Well, that makes me feel better.

Yep—50 years playing the piano to finally realize it's not primarily about playing the piano. It's about playing the love—*through* the piano!

Thank you for your help, and your words today. They will be stamped somewhere inside me to never forget again.

Good. Remember this: Just play *love*.

Let go of your over-concern about the notes, the virtuosity, the technical perfectionistic whatever. Just imagine that your whole purpose is to be a transmitter of *pure love*. One note at a time.

And the more you keep your intention focused on *that* objective, the fear and anxiety and neurosis and self-doubt—it all begins to fall away.

I will remember this.

Just like when the sun comes out after a rainy, cloudy day—you forget about the rain. You just bask in the sunshine.

And the sun is *always* there—even behind the clouds. That's what you need to remember.

Just play the love. Everything else is secondary.

Because when you breathe your last breath of this life—that's *all* that will really matter.

Thank you for your guidance. You cannot imagine how much it helps.

You're welcome.

Chapter 31

Reflections on Rhosymedre

The highest tribute to the dead is not grief but gratitude.

—THORNTON WILDER

VELVET.

That's what it was like.

If velvet had a sound, I heard it that Wednesday morning. From the very first note, when the tears began to flow and the tangible presence of love echoed throughout Highland Presbyterian Church.

It was Dallas Tidwell's memorial service. Thirty-five clarinetists seated together towards the front of the sanctuary. Former students, Louisville Orchestra members, colleagues from Dallas's own college days.

Theirs were the very first sounds heard as the service began.

But what they created was not simply the sound of a clarinet ensemble. Rather, there was a luminous, silken texture to the tone that transcended any single category of instrument.

As the plaintive, poignant melody of Vaughan William's "Rhosymedre" hymn ebbed and flowed like the rolling ocean waves of the English coast the composer knew so well, I was once again stunned by the sheer miracle that is music.

These 35 human beings, blowing into wooden cylinders with reeds on top and metal keys attached to the sides, all breathing, moving, thinking as one, their collective efforts vibrating the air, the synchronous sound waves traveling through the room, penetrating my physical body through ear and skin.

The fact that this acoustical phenomenon could somehow transmit even a portion of the immense love, caring, gratitude, and compassion felt by each one of these clarinetists who had been students of Dallas Tidwell—well, that felt miraculous to me.

Their love for Dallas infused every note. Their appreciation for him flowed directly from mind and heart through each instrument and every phrase, transmuted into the sonic velvet surging through the sanctuary, their memories of Dallas's role in their lives ensouled in sound.

Their singular intention to honor their teacher was exquisitely channeled through these particular notes, composed 75 years earlier by the son of a British preacher. The composer's love of folk music and of the common people reminded us of Dallas's fierce humility, honesty, and total dedication to teaching his students the music of life—even as they studied the life in music.

In some mysterious way that the human mind simply cannot comprehend, Dallas was there with us all, his spirit playing through each of the 35, a final gesture of love to all who loved him so.

PART VIII

In Tune with Teaching

UNLEASHING THE POTENTIAL

Chapter 32

In Three and a Half Hours, She Changed My Life Forever

Every child deserves a champion—an adult who will never give up on them, who understands the power of connection and insists that they become the best that they can possibly be.

—RITA PIERSON

I PLAY THE PIANO TODAY BECAUSE OF THIS WOMAN'S BELIEF in me.

"Oh, you like to improvise? That's wonderful. Did you know that Sylvia Rabinov improvises her cadenzas when she plays Mozart? You would enjoy hearing her."

Sparkling. Bright-eyed. Unfailingly encouraging. And so, so kind.

I absolutely blossomed in her presence. Never before had I encountered a piano teacher who seemed so delighted to help me learn. Never before had I encountered a piano teacher who welcomed so enthusiastically whatever I had to offer.

I was 15 years old, and I'd had good teachers in the past. But Janet Dubois somehow communicated her belief in my potential in such a way that I absolutely could not miss it, even if I tried.

I have never forward to piano lessons as much as I did that summer.

It was 1975 and I was attending summer session at Brevard Music Center. Brevard is considered the Tanglewood of the South. Every summer for seven weeks, this sleepy North Carolina town nestled in the Great Smoky Mountains becomes a hotbed of world-class music making, drawing hundreds of the nation's best young musicians, dozens of world-renowned faculty, and tens of thousands who enjoy over 80 performances ranging from chamber music to opera to symphonic masterpieces.

Piano was not my main instrument (I was there on a band scholarship and played baritone horn in the wind ensemble and concert band), and, although I was a decent pianist and good sight-reader, my innate musicality far outpaced my technical facility.

Because my piano playing left a lot to be desired, I felt far inferior to, and somewhat jealous of, those dozens of young pianists whose fingers flew across the keys, effortlessly executing passages that I could never hope to master.

But my relationship with the piano—and to music, for that matter—was to change forever that summer, thanks in no small part to Ms. Dubois.

"Now, let's try it without the pedal. And I want you to really listen to the relationship between the right and left hands, and let the left hand support that beautiful melody."

I play the piano today because of this woman's contagious enthusiasm.

Her name was pronounced *Doo-boyce*, not the more French sounding *Doo-bwah*, and she was a southern lady all the way. An instructor at Converse College, she had apparently been teaching at Brevard for a few years, usually working with the less-advanced students. (The piano majors got to study with the highfaluting teachers from Julliard and Curtis and other prestigious places.)

But Ms. Dubois made those of us who were not in the top echelon of future conservatory stars feel like stars in our own right.

What I remember most about our lessons was not the technical dimensions. I vaguely recall working a bit on matters of touch, articulation, pedaling, and the like.

But what touched me, and the reason why, 40 years later, I attribute my sticking with the piano in the first place to this diminutive, delightful woman, was her irrepressible, unyielding, and ebullient belief in my abilities.

I could see the enthusiasm written all over her face every time I walked into her studio for my lesson.

"Feel free to really bring out the contrast in this passage. No holding back. You can make it even more dramatic! That's much better. Beethoven would have liked that!"

I play the piano today because of this woman's deep commitment to calling forth my best self.

At some point during every lesson, she would ask me to improvise something. I complied with my pedestrian version of "Take Five" or "C Jam Blues," and she would respond as though Oscar Peterson or Art Tatum had granted her a private audience.

As we worked on the Chopin Polonaise C-sharp minor, she

would somehow build on the best of what I brought to the lesson, even in the midst of missed notes and awkward fingerings.

Every moment in our lessons felt like an adventure in affirmation, in finding the good and amplifying it.

I never, ever felt less than or looked down upon because my pianistic gifts were modest compared to all those conservatory-bound virtuosos who totally intimated me as I walked past row after row of the practice cabins on my way to and from the dorm.

"Now I know this looks hard, but it's just right for you. You will play this beautifully."

I play the piano today because of this woman's unflappable encouragement.

Since the camp lasted seven weeks, and I was not a piano major, I would receive a total of seven half-hour lessons. That anyone could have such an impact on my life in only three and one half hours of contact remains astonishing to me.

Such is the power of a teacher who dares to fall in love—with music, with life, and with the potential of those she serves.

Thank you, Ms. Dubois. Even now, you live in every note I play and in every student whose life I touch.

Chapter 33

Don't Delay, Say Thank You Today

One day you will wake up and there won't be any more time to do the things you've always wanted. Do it now.

—PAULO COELHO

HE WAS TALL, ELEGANT, DIGNIFIED, AND IN HIS MID-70S. I DID not expect to hear *this* man speak in *that* voice.

It was a cross between a squeak and a sore throat, sounding sort of like the eighth-grade boy who vacillates between soprano and bass within a single phrase.

When I first heard him, you could never have convinced me that Howard Swan was to become one of the most important and inspirational figures in my musical life.

It was the first day of a five-day summer symposium at Westminster Choir College. I was musically and professionally quite wet behind the ears, only 20 years old, attending summer school at Westminster because I was about to start my first full-time job.

Although I had no—zero—nada—experience (and at the time very little interest) in singing, directing choirs, or anything even remotely related to the world of vocal music, I had accepted a job as director of middle and upper school music at Rutgers Preparatory School in nearby Somerset, New Jersey.

The school had a solid and well-established music program in the elementary grades, thanks to the tireless efforts of the venerable Mary Alice Johnson. I was hired based on my enthusiasm and overall musical competency, plus my capacity to work alongside Mary Alice to build a solid music program in the middle and upper schools.

However, the choral area terrified me. I would be inheriting a madrigal group and middle school choir, along with the middle school band I would be conducting. Music history and appreciation classes made up the remainder of my duties.

I decided to do everything in my power to learn what I needed to learn before my very first day of my very first real job.

Westminster was the obvious place to spend my summer, since the school had a stellar reputation for choral excellence. The world-renowned Westminster Choir began on this very campus in Princeton, New Jersey, just up the road from my home in Somerset. Westminster's faculty directory read like a who's who in choral excellence at the time: Joseph Flummerfelt, Allen Crowell, Helen Kemp, and Frauke Hassemann. Robert Shaw was in residence there every summer. Westminster was undoubtedly the place to learn about choral music.

When I saw that the focus of Swan's workshop would be techniques for building choral sound—without having to actually demonstrate with one's own voice, I figured I'd hit the jackpot.

I could actually learn how to help my students sing well without having to depend on my own lack of experience, skill, and confidence in my own voice. That was exactly what I needed.

I had begun voice lessons a couple of weeks before, as soon as I accepted the job offer, but I was by no means progressing fast enough to feel self-assured in working with young singers.

So there I was, sitting in the bass section, eyes (and ears) riveted on the man with the squeaky voice. In spite of my reservations, I'd paid for this course in advance. Even if I didn't learn more than an exercise or two, I might as well stay around.

Then Dr. Swan began to tell his story. He talked about how his promising career as an operatic tenor was cut short when he contracted the polio that would paralyze one vocal cord and leave him unable to sing again. He told us how the dark night of the soul following this shattering of his dreams led him into the choral field and into his quest to discover just how he might help a choir create the sounds he could hear inside his own mind. He would have to do this without a vocal instrument that could model such a sound.

During those unforgettable, challenging, and inspiring five days, through countless exercises, stories, metaphors, and demonstrations, Dr. Swan evoked nuances of choral sound that I had never imagined possible without the aid of direct vocal modeling.

But these powerful lessons in molding good choral tone were the least of the gifts I received from Dr. Swan.

*   *   *

What I remember most vividly, these 35 years later, is his presence. His patience. His powerful use of story and metaphor to evoke not only the sound, but the emotional intensity and nuance required of each musical passage.

Howard Swan made me, a total beginner in the choral world,

feel as though I was part of something great, a union of hearts, minds, and souls dedicated to bringing forth the very essence of life itself through the medium of music.

This tall, aging man with the squeaky voice touched my heart as no teacher, mentor, or conductor before or since with his conviction, encyclopedic musical knowledge, and gentle yet commanding presence.

In spite of, or perhaps because of, the adversity he faced waking up that morning long ago with a paralyzed vocal cord, Dr. Swan called forth the greatness in each of us during that unforgettable week in July 1980.

Fifteen years later, in September 1995, living a life that felt light years away from my time at Rutgers Prep, I suddenly thought of Dr. Swan.

Overwhelmed with appreciation for his role in my life, I decided at that very moment to look him up, find his phone number, and call him, just to say thank you for how profoundly he impacted and inspired my musical and personal life.

I called the summer activities department at Westminster and asked if they could help me locate Dr. Swan. What I heard next broke my heart in two.

Howard Swan had passed away just one week before.

I had missed the opportunity to tell him thank you.

From that moment on, I stopped delaying when the impulse would emerge to reach out and say thank you to a mentor, teacher, or anyone else whose presence and impact had lightened my load.

This has been my practice for the past 20 years—in honor of Howard Swan.

Thank you, Dr. Swan.

Your legacy still lives.

Chapter 34

Why the Best Performers Can Sometimes Be Lousy Teachers

I have come to believe that a great teacher is a great artist
and that there are as few as there are any other great artists.
Teaching might even be the greatest of the arts
since the medium is the human mind and spirit.

—JOHN STEINBECK

FOR YEARS, I THOUGHT SOMETHING WAS WRONG WITH ME.
Let me share five encounters with former teachers (I've changed
minor details to protect the guilty). Five sets of instructions that
were absolutely wrong, even detrimental to me as a music student.

"You're clearly not making progress. Are you practicing? Are
you putting in the time?"

I was both incensed and humiliated. Not only had I put in
the time, I had been working on this same left-hand passage in

this same Chopin prelude for three solid weeks, coming back week after week to my lesson with this supposedly top teacher from a prestigious music conservatory, and I was not getting better.

She insisted that I wasn't doing the work. I was doing the work, but she did not know how to help me solve the specific musical problem I was struggling with. She couldn't crack my individual learning code. But she couldn't admit that. She had to blame me for not working hard enough.

"Just go to the 'space' and let the music flow from there."

No, I'm sorry. I have practiced going to this space for years and the only problem with it is, even though I can hear music inside me when I'm in that space, what I play just doesn't come out sounding anything like it. I can hang out in this state of consciousness all day long, and unless I can accurately translate what I am hearing inside my head, the space won't do me much good.

This brilliant teacher was born with perfect pitch, and had no need to translate the sounds in his head into notes on the piano. He knew what notes to play. His advice was valuable, but incomplete.

"I don't want you to take notes. My (famous) teacher at (prestigious) conservatory didn't let us take notes. We had to pay close attention."

I was playing close attention. One of the things I discovered through analyzing my own learning style was that note taking actually increases both my comprehension and my retention. It's one of the reasons I have been keeping journals since 1980. Taking notes actually helps me learn.

He was stuck in his own methods, and he imposed the same approach on every student. It didn't work for me. At all. Still doesn't—35 years later.

"Just play. You'll figure it out."

No, I won't figure it out. That's why I came to you in the first place. Here's the problem I'm facing. Here's what I've tried. Here's the result I've achieved. What do you think I need to do? When you tell me to "just play" week after week, it only adds to my frustration. Oh, well. I will have to figure it out for myself.

"I don't think we need to look at that. My approach will be just fine for you. You just need to apply yourself more."

Actually, the reason I brought this book, *Indispensables of Piano Playing*, by Abby Whiteside, into my lesson was that I've had a feeling ever since I first read it that this innovative approach might hold the key to the technical breakthrough I've been searching for. I'm sorry you're not even open to discussing it.

(I discovered two decades later that I was right, when I found a teacher who trained with one of Whiteside's students. Everything changed for me from that moment on.)

*   *   *

Five teachers, each incredibly gifted in his or her own right, who, because of their very giftedness and their paths to proficiency, were constitutionally unable and emotionally unwilling to take the time to figure out how their student (me) needed to learn.

Of course, it eventually worked out for the good. After all, that's why I do what I do.

I learned what I could from them.

But most importantly, I learned to teach myself and also to find guides and mentors along the way who could help me crack my own unique learning code.

But it was painful to go through. Over and over, teacher after teacher, not understanding how I needed to learn. And something in me knew all along that I was getting bad advice, even though it was coming from high-prestige people in high-prestige situations who were highly regarded as performers.

Then I started to notice this same pattern among students who came to me, often after studying with others who couldn't quite crack their learning codes.

They were often frustrated, beating themselves up for not being good enough, trying hard enough, practicing enough.

But as I got to know them, I realized it was not their fault.

Not at all. They were just dutifully following the misguided instructions of the former prodigy, who although proficient themselves, were often worse than clueless about what the ordinary person whose gift did not bloom so early really needed in order to learn and thrive.

Then I wondered—does this pattern occur in other areas besides music? Great athletes who became not-so-great coaches. Great performers, actors, and artists who choose to teach, but whose students rarely excel at the highest levels.

I started to see it everywhere.

These gifted performers who became less-than-effective coaches, mentors, or teachers, all shared an identical blind spot.

I call it the pitfall of prodigy pedagogy. Simply stated, it's an inability to accurately see all the steps that may be necessary in order to get from point A to point B.

You see the naturally gifted, prodigious talent in any field tends not to know how they got there. They are consumed with a desire for mastery in their chosen field, and pursue that mastery with a deep and unrelenting passion. The only downside is this. Their own early-blooming proficiency blinds them to the one thing that could help them help others excel.

The prodigy not only has developed habits that they are unaware of, but because they are unaware of the habits they have developed, they literally can no longer see the path by which they developed the habits.

Here's how it translates to the teaching and learning process.

It's like the teachers took a jet plane from LA to Chicago. They are trying to tell you how to get there. The only problem is, you are driving a pickup truck.

You have never been on a jet.

Yet they talk to you in aeronautic terms; get frustrated when you ask about road signs, and accuse you of not working hard enough when you've been driving all night.

They think you're lazy, and you begin to think you're crazy.

*   *   *

Here's my advice to former prodigies who teach.

First, open up to the possibility that you might not be as great a teacher as you think, and that you just might need to work a bit harder to help the students who do not make the kind of progress you made as a student.

If you have perfect pitch, stop assuming you know what other people experience when they try to make music, compose, or transcribe. You don't. You are not wired in the same way. Your advice is far less relevant than someone who actually had to develop their ears through trial and error, effort and diligence.

If you are a natural athlete, please think twice before you become a coach. You probably have forgotten what it feels like to be a beginner, starting out awkward and clumsy, building skills and smoothness over time. Even if you've taken the same sequence of steps towards mastery, for you those steps may be unconsciously internalized, and your assumptions about what others need to progress may be completely wrong.

If you were a prodigy as a musician, you probably have no clue what less "talented" students really need in order to learn to do what easily came to you. Dare to learn from your students. Seek to discover the conditions under which they learn best. Talk to colleagues who have struggled to attain that which comes easily to you to find out more about their process of learning. Learn from them.

If you are a natural communicator, telling stories around the dinner table and giving speeches since you were five, please don't teach public speaking—at least not yet. Although you may be world-class, your unconscious competency probably will block you from seeing the steps that others who are less proficient may have to go through to get to the pinnacle that you reached so early.

Don't teach people in the areas that have come easily to you—unless you are willing to take the time and effort to fully confront the pitfalls of prodigy pedagogy.

Otherwise, at the very least, you will probably do them a disservice. You might even discourage or damage them forever. And your arrogance, impatience, and insistence that your way is the right way might be slaughtering their spirits.

Stop it.

If you're a student and you happen to be under the tutelage of a former prodigy who exhibits any of these characteristics, initiate a conversation wherein you explore what you've discovered about how you learn best.

Consider sharing and discussing this chapter.

And continue with diligence and determination to find both the methods and the guides that will best serve your unique journey on the path towards mastery.

Chapter 35

Star-Spangled Possibility

The conductor must breathe life into the score.

—CHARLES MUNCH

WHAT I REMEMBER MOST ABOUT HIM WAS HIS INTENSITY.

Georgia All-State Band, my junior year. I was first chair euphonium in a massive ensemble of more than two hundred students from all across the state.

The diminutive Joe Barry Mullins was our guest conductor for these three days of intense rehearsal and performance.

I loved all-state bands. The quality of musicianship was always outstanding and there are few thrills greater than performing great music with high-caliber musicians.

I had worked under several exceptional and highly skilled conductors before—Jamie Hafner and Robert Barr at Brevard, Roger Heath in the American Musical Ambassadors Band, Vic Zajac in our regional clinic bands—all legends in the world of band excellence.

However, Dr. Mullins operated on a different level.

Never before had I encountered a conductor with such unbridled intensity and sheer passion for the music.

Never before had I observed someone who was so utterly present to his internal sense of the sound that he could convey so much through the raising of an eyebrow, a minimal gesture with his baton, or even a simple glance in your direction.

The piece that took me—and the entire ensemble—to a place I had never dreamed possible was Luigi Zaninelli's arrangement of the "Star-Spangled Banner." This unique setting of our national anthem features dark sonorous textures, skillful juxtaposition of "America the Beautiful," and a stunning, majestic climax.

Dr. Mullins would sing along, groan, moan, and grunt as he conducted, his essential musicality seeming to burst forth so powerfully that he could hardly contain himself.

As we rehearsed Zaninelli's stunning recreation of this familiar melody, I can hear his voice now—More! Intensity! More! In-ten-sity!

We gave all that we had and then gave still more.

It wasn't about volume or how loud we were playing, although the passage was marked fortissimo.

It was about our quality of presence, of focus, of—intensity.

And the result was breathtaking.

"The Star-Spangled Banner" began to sing itself.

During the performance, it seemed that every possible feeling of positive connection to one's national heritage—pride, joy, brotherhood, elation, freedom, the sense of victory—flooded through the hearts and minds and bodies and souls of everyone present.

A single pulse beat through all the performers and the hundreds more in attendance—a pulse of patriotism and pride and passion and power.

Great conductors—the truly great ones—inspire in us capacities and latencies that we never imagined were there, calling forth levels of accomplishment that moments before seemed out of reach.

They uplift our spirits, up level our standards, uproot our self-doubt, and upgrade our self-esteem.

And for years, for decades, for a lifetime, they leave an imprint of possibility that forever leads us into realizing more and more of the greatness, the goodness, the grace that is ever available in each moment of music—and every moment of life.

Thank you, Dr. Mullins.

Chapter 36

Just One Page

*Be as careful of the books you read as of the
company you keep; for your habits and character will be
as much influenced by the former as by the latter.*

—PAXTON HOOD

HE COULD NEVER HAVE KNOWN.

I was attending a month-long jazz piano workshop at North
Texas State University.

It was the summer of 1979. I was between colleges.

I had spent my first two years at Davidson College where I
made a futile but sincere attempt to be a premed major.

After I realized I was spending at least three times as much
time in the music building than the biology lab, it became clear
that I needed to make a change.

I decided on Rutgers University for two reasons: one, I would
be close to the jazz mecca that was New York City; and two, I
would have the opportunity to study with virtuoso jazz pianist
Kenny Barron, who was teaching at Rutgers at the time.

I wanted to get a head start on what I knew would be an
intense two years of jazz study. So I signed up for Dan Haerle's
jazz piano workshop.

Dan was a legend in the jazz education world. He, along
with David Baker, Jerry Coker, and Jamey Aebersold, pioneered

the codification and theoretical analysis that would ultimately make the language of jazz accessible to countless thousands of aspiring amateur and professional musicians.

The workshop was outstanding, as was the environment. North Texas State University, even in the summer, was brimming with top-flight musicianship. Plus, the many taco stands in Denton served delicious Mexican food on a budget that worked for me.

* * *

On the very last day of class, Dan gave it away almost as an afterthought.

"By the way, this is just a list of some books that have been valuable to me. There are books on music as well as other topics. You might enjoy checking some of these out. These have been valuable in my journey; you might find them valuable to you, too."

I quickly glanced at the list and saw a few titles I was familiar with. Most, however were new to me.

What I found fascinating was that most of the books on the list were not about music at all. They focused on philosophy, spirituality, psychology—all exploring the ultimate human quest: how to live a life of meaning, purpose, contribution, and fulfillment.

I was pleasantly surprised to receive such a list at the end of a music workshop. I would soon discover that the very best musicians, particularly those who dare to commit to the improvisers' path, were often practical philosophers, deep thinkers, and explorers of innovative ideas outside of the musical realm.

When class ended, I went back to the airport and boarded the plane that would take me back to my home in Brunswick, Georgia, where would I stay for the final few weeks before my trip across the country to a new life in New Jersey.

One of the first books listed looked interesting. *There Is a River: The Story of Edgar Cayce.*

I wondered what this was about. Who was Edgar Cayce? I would start with this book. It would give me something to do besides practice over the next few weeks.

When I got home, I visited the local Barnes & Noble, the biggest bookstore in town, and was pleasantly surprised to find *There Is a River.*

Over the next week, I immersed myself in the story of this remarkable man whose unusual intuitive gift led him into a remarkable life of spiritual exploration and service to humanity.

My mind was transformed into a new dimension.

I was astonished to read the stories of Cayce's readings and life experiences, but most significantly, the book opened a new door in my own awareness because of his obvious and unshakeable search for truth.

Learning about Cayce's life changed my own. This book confirmed many of my own intuitions regarding the spiritual journey and about my own individual ability to connect with and communicate directly with the indwelling inner source of wisdom, without the need of an external mediator or other authority.

There were other books on the list, including *Autobiography of a Yogi* by Paramahansa Yogananda, Richard Bach's *Jonathan Livingston Seagull*, and perhaps a dozen more. I ultimately read nearly all of them.

Mr. Haerle had opened the door to two brand-new worlds

for me: the world of jazz piano theory and this new domain of spiritual philosophy that shone brightly through each word in every book I chose from his list.

* * *

Many years later, I realized the true gift of this experience.

Those of us who have the privilege to teach and mentor adolescents and young adults wield more influence than we might imagine.

Why? Because at that time in a young person's life cycle, one mentor, one book, even one conversation can alter the trajectory of an entire life.

This occurred for me simply as a result of Mr. Haerle handing me a simple list of books he found inspiring.

Years later, when I became Dan's colleague and peer at the Aebersold Jazz Workshops, I thanked him profusely for that sheet of paper.

I don't know if he ever fully understood what a difference it made, but at least I felt I had completed the circle of appreciation.

Since then I have often shared my own personal booklist with my students, workshop participants, and even concert audiences.

What a beautiful example of the power of a single action to transform a life.

Thank you, Dan.

Keep handing out those lists.

Chapter 37

She Always Said Yes

A word of encouragement from a teacher to a child can change a life. A word of encouragement from a spouse can save a marriage. A word of encouragement from a leader can inspire a person to reach [his or her] potential.

—JOHN C. MAXWELL

"MISS TOLBERT, I'D LIKE TO WRITE AN ARRANGEMENT FOR THE band."

"I think that's a great idea, Harry!"

"Miss Tolbert, I want to try out for drum major."

"I think you should do it."

"Miss Tolbert, could we use the band room to rehearse after school?"

"Of course. When do you want it?"

Patti Tolbert, my band director at Glynn County Junior High School, always said yes.

Yes to my requests.

Yes to my curiosity.

Yes to my potential.

I was a gangly, extremely tall kid from Brunswick Georgia.

I was shy, awkward but madly in love with music. I had been switched to baritone horn from trumpet in seventh grade, and from the minute I arrived on the GCJHS campus, Miss Tolbert took me under her wing.

When I caught pressure from the school's coach to go out for the basketball team, I had a talk with Miss Tolbert.

"I don't want to play basketball. Do you think I should?"

"I think you need to do what feels right to you. You have a lot of musical ability. You can develop that. You don't have to play a sport if that's not what you want."

"Thank you. You know, you're right. I don't have to do that. I've felt a lot of pressure from the coach, but my heart's not in it. I'm going to tell him no."

Luckily, saying no to the coach opened a door to the next yes that aligned with my gifts and passions.

The very next week, I became drum major for the Glynn County Junior High Marching Band. It was a much better choice than center for the basketball team.

I was lucky, because my mom and my grandfather both agreed—no basketball unless I wanted to do it. My father was long gone, and grandmother had died when I was in the seventh grade, so these two were my whole family.

Plus, I never had the slightest interest in basketball. I enjoyed playing baseball, and listening to the Atlanta Braves games with my grandpa on the radio. And of course, I loved our school football games and playing in the marching band. But that was about it as far as my interest in sports. My passions belonged to music and academic subjects.

So Miss Tolbert's simple act of telling this 14-year-old, six-foot-nine-inch kid that he didn't have to be anybody but himself made a bigger difference than I could have imagined.

* * *

During my eighth-grade year, I got the idea that I would like to learn how to write music for a band. I loved the song "We've Only Just Begun," and thought I could learn how to write for the instruments by arranging this song for concert band.

When I told Miss Tolbert, she was thrilled, and, after looking at what I'd written, invited me to conduct my very own arrangement at the spring concert.

I was excited beyond imagination.

My very first attempt to bring the music inside me to the outside.

I was only just beginning, and what a blessing to have a teacher who simply said yes to my initiative. Who said yes to hard work. Who said yes to the slightest hint of talent. Who said yes to my possibilities.

* * *

Fast-forward two years: I was a sophomore at Glynn Academy, the high school just across the way.

"Harry, I think you would benefit from a summer at Brevard Music Center. There is a scholarship available for band students and I believe you would qualify."

It didn't matter that I was no longer in her class. Miss Tolbert kept me in her mind and stayed on the lookout for opportunities to support this tall and gangly euphonium player who was absolutely crazy about music.

The summer at Brevard was to transform my life forever. Seven weeks of constant immersion in world-class music making, exposure to outstanding high school and college musicians, and the opportunity to go to concerts featuring the world's premier concert artists every single night of the summer. And all I had to do was show up. And show up I did.

I thoroughly immersed myself in every possible opportunity.

And Patti Tolbert didn't have to do any of that. After all, I was just another kid from South Georgia. She personally had absolutely nothing to gain by going out of her way to get me a full scholarship. I wasn't even in her class anymore. No reason to do it—except because she believed in me.

* * *

Those seven weeks at Brevard in 1975 became the single most transformational summer of my life.

All thanks to a teacher who sought opportunity for her students and made the choice to open doors of possibility for them to walk through.

My two years in the Glynn County Junior High School Band molded my musical and personal character more than I realized.

If you're a teacher, be a Patti Tolbert. A teacher who says yes to possibility for her students. A teacher who says yes to opening doors of opportunity. A teacher who says yes to her students' futures.

Thank you, Miss Tolbert, for always saying yes.

Chapter 38

Captain of His Soul

God tells me how the music should sound,
but you stand in the way.
—ARTURO TOSCANINI

HIS EYES MET MINE AND FOR THAT INSTANT, I COULD BARELY breathe.

I broke out in a cold sweat, this strange synthesis of terror and ecstasy riding on the soaring waves of this peak moment of Wagner's sonorous masterpiece.

"Elsa's Procession to the Cathedral." Brevard Music Center Wind Ensemble. Summer 1975.

He sat in the wheelchair facing us, gripping the baton with his gnarled fingers, unable to speak a single word, his eyes, gestures, and grunts his sole means of communicating the power and beauty of this magnificent work. I thought of William Ernest Henley's poem "Invictus."

Out of the night that covers me,
Black as the pit from pole to pole,
I thank whatever gods may be
For my unconquerable soul.

It was the final concert of the summer season, and Dr. Robert Barr was our guest conductor.

Dr. Barr was a legend. Graduate of Cincinnati Conservatory, winner of national competitions as tuba soloist, and 36 years as band director of award-winning marching and symphonic bands.

He was also a firm disciplinarian. Some would say tyrannical, in the tradition of Toscanini.

He suffered no fools, and often would mete out pushups as punishment for the slightest infractions during marching band practice.

But no more.

Once he had been an imposing figure, standing six foot four with a wingspan that seemed to take the entire band in his arms.

Now this mighty eagle slumped and drooled before us.

In the fell clutch of circumstance
I have not winced nor cried aloud.
Under the bludgeonings of chance
My head is bloody, but unbowed.

The stroke had partially paralyzed him, and he could speak only in grunts.

He had some use of his right hand, and wielded his baton with awkward precision.

But the betrayal of his body could not extinguish the fire in his eyes, the passion in his heart, or the relentless drive for musical excellence that had made him a legend.

Robert Barr was known throughout the South to all who loved band music.

For many years, he directed the Glynn Academy symphonic and marching bands, decades before I would attend the school.

Barr was known as a firm and intimidating band director, one who was often more feared and respected than loved.

His results were undeniable. His bands consistently won state, regional, and even national awards. I once sat astonished as I listened to a live recording of the Glynn Academy High School band, under Barr's direction, playing an intricate transcription of Bach's "Toccata and Fugue in D Minor."

Barr lived, breathed, ate, and drank music. It was his life, his reason for being. And his dutiful wife Annie was always there, right beside him, her calm demeanor the perfect complement to his fierce intensity.

And then the stroke.

Beyond this place of wrath and tears
Looms but the horror of the shade,
And yet the menace of the years
Finds, and shall find me, unafraid.

We didn't know what to expect. Mr. Barr was known to be volatile. On more than one occasion, he threw his baton at a band member in a moment of frustration.

And our one rehearsal of "Elsa's Procession" with him was difficult at best. We did our very best to follow his gestures, but in the moments when it was obvious that we could not read his mind and interpret his awkward signals, we could see the rage blazing in his eyes.

If this man could have jumped out of his wheelchair in that moment, I could imagine the entire wind ensemble running and screaming in terror.

But I could not fathom what it would be like to have a fully functioning mind and brilliant musical intellect locked in a body that could no longer express even a fraction of its former might.

> *It matters not how strait the gate*
> *How charged with punishments the scroll*
> *I am the master of my fate*
> *I am the captain of my soul.*

I have never been so close to tears while performing. Every awkward, jagged movement of Mr. Barr's baton-wielding hand seemed to evoke an emotional power and passion that was almost overwhelming. Every crescendo and decrescendo was filled with meaning.

I was playing my heart out for this man who could barely move his arm, yet whose very presence was drawing out from all of us the performance of a lifetime.

All of him was right there with us. Only the physical ability to articulate the vastness within was missing. But we caught it anyhow.

Robert Barr would not be deterred.

Wagner's Elsa arrived at the cathedral with her beauty and poise, dignity and power fully intact, gallantly escorted by a man whose indomitable spirit could never be confined to his now-broken body.

> *It matters not how strait the gate*
> *How charged with punishments the scroll*
> *I am the master of my fate*
> *I am the captain of my soul.*

Thank you, Dr. Barr.

What is the calling of the musician?
I believe it is to become a living,
breathing human instrument for
the transmission of love.

—**HARRY PICKENS**